CROSLEY

And Crosley Motors

An Illustrated History of America's First Compact Car and the Company that Built it.

Michael Banks

Iconografix

Iconografix
1830A Hanley Road
Hudson, Wisconsin 54016 USA

Library of Congress Control Number: 2012931304

ISBN-13: 978-1-58388-293-1
ISBN10: 1-58388-293-6

Printed in The United States of America

Book Proposals

Iconografix is a publishing company specializing in books for transportation enthusiasts. We publish in a number of different areas, including Automobiles, Auto Racing, Buses, Construction Equipment, Emergency Equipment, Farming Equipment, Railroads & Trucks. The Iconografix imprint is constantly growing and expanding into new subject areas.

Authors, editors, and knowledgeable enthusiasts in the field of transportation history are invited to contact the Editorial Department at Iconografix, 1830A Hanley Rd., Hudson, WI 54016

The Crosley Automobile Club hosts regional and national meets, publishes a quarterly magazine, and provides help and advice with technical problems. It also maintains an extensive collection of reference material.

You can contact the Crosley Automobile Club by mail at:
Crosley Automobile Club Inc.
307 Schaeffer Rd
Blandon, PA 19510

or at its home on the Web:
http://crosleyautoclub.com/

In addition, Yahoo! Groups hosts the Crosley Car Owner's Club, which offers message boards, photos and other resources:
http://autos.groups.yahoo.com/group/Crosley/

CONTENTS

Preface   *My First Crosley*   4

Introduction   *At The Peak*   6

Chapter 1   *1907-1914: The First Crosley Automobiles*   8

Chapter 2   *1915-1934: Huckster and Inventor*   16

Chapter 3   *1935-1940: The Car of Tomorrow*   23

Chapter 4   *1941-1944: Wartime*   48

Chapter 5   *1945-1947: A New Start*   70

Chapter 6   *1948-1949: Flying High*   88

Chapter 7   *1950: Competition and Additions*   109

Chapter 8   *1951-1952: The End*   116

PREFACE

My First Crosley

My first encounter with a Crosley automobile was at the age of four. My parents rented a house in the Cincinnati suburb of Milford, Ohio, on a well-kept street of stately old homes. Behind us was a rather smallish house with a smallish car in the driveway, owned by a couple named Griswold.

This was the middle of the 1950s, and as young as I was I paid attention to automobiles (or, as older people called them back then, "machines"). In my mind's eye I can still see the torpedo back of a Chevrolet, the curves of a Studebaker, the hump of a Dodge. But the one that's really engraved in memory is a 1951 Crosley station wagon—and for a very special reason.

Crosley fans know that in 1951 and 1952 Crosley Motors offered a distinctive feature on its "Super"

models: a propeller mounted on the bullet nose of the car's grille. This propeller was my point of interaction with that Crosley station wagon. Every chance I got I ran across the yards and spun that propeller into a blur.

Several decades after encountering my first Crosley, I spun the propeller on another Crosley, this time at the Crosley Automobile Club's annual meet in Wauseon, Ohio. The encounter prompted me to search out the owner of that 1951 Crosley-next-door, Jack Griswold. I found him retired in Florida and learned that he was more than someone who had once owned a Crosley. Jack was a real Crosley enthusiast; he had owned a total of 14 different Crosleys in the 1950s and '60s. Jack also gave me a photo of that '51 wagon, which you can see here. (It was then that I learned that it was, in fact, a 1951 Super.)

So I have Jack Griswold to thank for setting me on the road to becoming a Crosley enthusiast and writing this book. My enthusiasm wasn't confined to Crosley autos. Like many people, my grandparents gave pride of place in their living room to one of the elaborate console model Crosley radios. The first radio station I tuned in with the tiny crystal set I put together in 1958 was Crosley's WLW, its tower only 30 miles from my home. The earliest television programs I watched emanated from Crosley Broadcasting's WLWT. And relics of the once-mighty Crosley empire—like the Shelvador refrigerator and Sav-A-Maid washer and dryer—filled the homes of friends and relatives as I was growing up. Some still do, for that matter, even though production of the original Crosley appliance line ceased in 1956. All that exposure eventually resulted in my researching and chronicling the Crosley story in magazines, TV and radio broadcasts, and elsewhere.

Of the many Crosley items I have avidly collected, I have never owned a Crosley automobile. I've ridden in and driven a few, and admired more. Those collector cars I've owned have mostly been major makes—Fords and Dodges from the 1950s and '60s. There are many more of those available than Crosleys, and Crosleys for sale tend to be snapped up quickly. Probably the closest I've come to owning a Crosley is a 1959 Nash Metropolitan, a car that you may be surprised to learn has a small connection with the Crosley…

But I'm getting ahead of myself. The purpose of this book is to provide a solid history of Crosley Motors and the Crosley automobile—its antecedents, evolution and eventual fate. Along with the history I offer anecdotes and previously-unpublished information about Crosley Motors and its founder. I also dispel the odd myth. On occasion, history's records and witnesses have left gaps in the story; those are bridged by gentle speculation, identified as such. All of this is illustrated with photos of various Crosley vehicles, plus ephemerae such as advertising.

I hope you enjoy reading this close-up of the Crosley as much as I enjoyed putting it together. Several folks have provided invaluable information, answers to odd questions, and visual and other material. These include Bill Angert, Jr., Dave Anspach, Keith Beecher, Alan Bent, Tom Boatner, Jim Bollman, Steve Cowdin, Clyde Haehnle, Norm Luppino, Tom Miller, Bill Myers, Diana McClure, John P. Olberholtze, Lou Rugani, and Paul van Vort. Thanks again to you all!

Certain institutions also have been helpful, among them: the Airborne & Special Operations Museum, Fayetteville, North Carolina (asomf.org); the Mighty 8th Air Force Heritage Museum outside Savannah, Georgia (mightyeighth.org); the Cincinnati Museum Center (cincymuseum.org); the Library of Virginia (lva. virginia.gov); the Public Library of Cincinnati & Hamilton County (cincinnatilibrary.org); and the Sarasota Classic Car Museum in Sarasota, Florida (sarasotacarmuseum.org).

In such a complex history, with events that span more than a century, it is possible that some errors have crept in. If so, they are my responsibility.

Michael A. Banks
Cincinnati, Ohio
June 2011

Photo by Bill Angert

INTRODUCTION
At the Peak

On Thursday, May 9, 1946, a small gray sedan sat at the head of a line of similar cars in a cavernous plant in Marion, Indiana. Surrounded by an anxious group of company officials, newsmen, local businessmen and other dignitaries, the automobile was the first of a brand-new line.

New car rollouts weren't unusual in Indiana, which had seen dozens over the preceding fifty years. But this car, the Crosley, drew more national attention than any car since the Ford Model A. It had the distinction of being the first new car available to the public since 1942, when civilian automotive production ceased in the wake of the United States' entry into World War II.

Those gathered for the ceremony took their time examining the car. A compact auto with a diminutive 59-pound engine, the Crosley promised as much as 50 miles to a gallon of gasoline—a not unimportant consideration in an era of gas rationing. Equally important,

the Crosley's price of $749 (set by the Federal Office of Price Control) was lower than that of any other production car in America.

The car's creator, Cincinnati industrialist Powel Crosley, Jr., stood quietly by, obviously proud of his achievement. Guest speaker Mayor James Garfield Stewart of Cincinnati briefly addressed the crowd, summing up Crosley's career and noting his accomplishments before introducing the industrialist. Crosley spoke about the car's positive public reception and thanked his brother, Lewis, and other Crosley executives.

As he spoke, Alice Cox, the wife of a prominent Marion businessman, waited in the driver's seat of the new car. At a nod from Crosley, she pressed the starter button. The starter motor engaged and the engine turned over, but failed to catch. A nervous chuckle went through the crowd as Crosley signaled Cox to try again. Again it failed to start. Cox touched the button

Christening of the first 1946 Crosley. Page Crosley Kess, Powel Crosley, Jr.'s daughter, smashes a bottle of champagne against the car's front bumper as Crosley, the Mayor of Cincinnati, and Crosley Motors executives and Lewis Crosley look on. *Banks Collection*

a third time, pressed the gas pedal, and it roared into life—much to the delight and relief of those present. To applause and cheers, Mrs. Cox drove the car off the line and into history, its engine purring.

The genesis of this moment was over forty years earlier, in 1898, when Powel Crosley, Jr. first aspired to become an automaker. At the age of twelve he decided to build an automobile because he was convinced that the few motorcars that cruised the streets in his home town of College Hill (a Cincinnati suburb) represented the wave of the future. In emulation of those marvels, Crosley enlisted his younger brother, Lewis, to help him add an electric motor, drive chain and steering mechanism to an abandoned buckboard wagon. He also borrowed eight dollars from Lewis to finance the venture. The boys' father, Powel Crosley, Sr., was amused by the project and promised young Powel a ten-dollar reward if his automobile worked.

This first Crosley car met the challenge by traversing a city block. The junior Crosley accepted the ten dollars, repaid his brother and the pair split the two-dollar profit. This was more exciting than going to a Cincinnati Reds game or hunting and fishing, his favorite activities. And it was only the beginning; from that day on Powel Crosley, Jr. was determined to become an automobile manufacturer, no matter what. And he would become wealthy.

At the time, Crosley was sure that he would make his fortune as an automobile manufacturer, rather than

A sketch made from memory by Powel Crosley, Jr. It represents the "electric car" he and his brother made from an old buckboard wagon. The front cover was decorative, and the steering gear completely exposed. An electric motor and battery were mounted in the box beneath the seat. The illustration appeared in the May 29, 1934, issue of *Youth's Companion* magazine, and was probably touched up by the magazine's art director. *Youth's Companion*

have to get rich before he could build automobiles. As any Crosley enthusiast (automobile or radio) will tell you, Crosley made millions by introducing the world's first affordable radio receiver in 1921, followed by what would become the world's most powerful radio station, WLW. These accomplishments laid the foundation for the broadcast industry, and Crosley became known as "the Henry Ford of Radio."

In 1898, the year of his first automotive success, Powel Crosley, Jr. was over two decades away from that fortune, and twice as far from putting the first Crosley-badged auto on the nation's highways. The route to his fortune would be circuitous, with several stops along the way to build automobiles.

"The only reason he became rich," said Lewis Crosley on more than one occasion, "was so he could build automobiles."

Hood ornament proclaiming "Crosley – A Fine Car." *Banks collection*

CHAPTER 1
1907-1914:
The First Crosley Automobiles

Powel Crosley, Jr., was a compulsive tinkerer in his youth. Born in 1886, he experimented with electricity, disassembled household gadgets and investigated just about every sort of technology available in those pre-radio days. But more than anything else the young Crosley was completely smitten with the automobile. He tried to convince his father to buy an automobile for the family, to no avail. (Cincinnati streetcar service was just fine as far as the elder Crosley was concerned. Besides, he was heavily invested in street railways.)

So it was left to Crosley to satisfy his automotive yearnings from afar. Throughout high school he kept up with the latest automotive developments by reading magazines like *Automobile Topics* and *The Motor*, and gazed longingly at every motorcar that passed. The occasional opportunity to look over a parked car must have been a real treat. He devoted endless hours to creating specifications and drawings of dream autos.

On graduating from high school in 1904, Crosley was set to attend the University of Cincinnati. His father, a moderately well-to-do attorney who was footing the bill, wanted him to study law. Young Crosley wasn't enthusiastic over the prospect. He found a summer job as a part-time chauffeur, to be close to automobiles, and thought about it. At the last minute he defiantly entered the university's engineering program.

Although this was no surprise to his friends, it was an unpleasant one for his father. The decision soon proved to be unpleasant for Powel Crosley, Jr., as well. He hadn't done well in math and science in high school and found himself close to flunking out after just a few months. He switched to law school early in 1905 and slogged his way through boring classes, working a summer job selling advertising. Then, in the spring of 1906, he decided to take his own path in life. He left college.

Crosley found a job selling municipal bonds for Rudolph Kleybolte & Co., owned by the father of a friend. Near year's end he abruptly left the company. It may have been no coincidence that at the same time Kleybolte's company was beginning to sink into a morass of financial and legal troubles. But Crosley maintained otherwise, later declaring that he left the job because he had decided it was time for him to "take a swing at the world."

His swing at the world would take the form of an automobile whose design he had been developing for some time. He called it the Marathon Six. It would be a six-cylinder car in an era when more autos were driven by four-cylinder engines than any other type. (In a survey of 133 1905 automobile models, 59 had four-cylinder engines, and 54 had two-cylinder engines. Eight-, six-, three-, and single-cylinder autos made up the rest of the group.)

Intended for the low end of the luxury car market, the Marathon Six would sell for $1,700 in a field that started at $2,000. He had no money, so Crosley went looking for investors. (According to Crosley, his father was adamant in his opposition to the venture, and thus wouldn't have helped him.) A very persuasive Powel Crosley, Jr., raised $10,000 from men in the legal, banking and other professions. It was quite a feat in an era when $10 was a good week's wage. But the automobile industry was the coming thing then. It promised big returns to anyone savvy enough to get in on the ground floor. It seemed as if investors everywhere were getting in on the action. Why not get a piece of it now, before the opportunity went away?

The Marathon Six Automobile Company began operation in the summer of 1907, but not in Cincinnati. Instead, Crosley went to work in a facility in Connersville, Indiana, a small town sixty miles from Cincinnati. He never said why, but the move certainly gave him privacy and put distance between him and his investors. These were important to a man like Crosley who didn't like to answer to anyone else.

Connersville had been the home of buggy and furniture makers for decades, and in recent years a number of these establishments had turned to building automobile bodies and other components. Connersville's Central Manufacturing, for example, had been making wood auto bodies for Cadillac for several years, and would eventually build steel bodies for Cord and Auburn.

Crosley set his salary at $12.50 per week and the new auto took shape. No photos or drawings survive, but we know from Crosley that the car's wheelbase was 114 inches, and that it was an "assembled car," which meant he would buy all the components—frame, engine, body, etc.—readymade from specialty manufacturers. Knowing some of the conventions of the auto industry and design at the time, we can speculate as to what the Marathon Six was like.

Its foundation would have been a steel frame. Pressed steel frames were the newest thing, and more than half the companies in the auto business were using them. Wood and armored wood frames could not match steel for strength.

The wheelbase and the axle track, or distance between tire tread centers, would in part dictate the size of the frame. The standard track back then was 56 inches, wide enough to match the ruts worn into most dirt roads by horse-drawn vehicles. So it's not a stretch to imagine the Marathon Six as having a 56-inch track to go along with its 114-inch wheelbase. (As a basis for comparison, the contemporary Ford Explorer's wheelbase is 114 inches, with a 59-inch track.) Not incidentally, the wheelbase and track of Henry Ford's new six-cylinder Model K measured 114 by 56 inches, too. Crosley was already an admirer of Ford, and Ford's design may have influenced Crosley's.

The Marathon Six would have rolled on artillery wheels, like nearly every auto of the time. Short, thick, hardwood spokes could handle the sharp lateral stresses of a heavy, high-powered auto, whereas long-spoked wood carriage wheels and thin wire bicycle wheels could not. Heavy metal spokes and stamped metal disc wheels were still a few years off.

Wheel diameter was a topic of much disagreement among automakers and owners. Automobile wheels were smaller than most carriage wheels, running anywhere from 24 to 42 inches in diameter. It is likely that Crosley went with smaller wheels, for a couple of reasons. First, smaller wheels gave an automobile a lower center of gravity, a vote for safety and handling. Second, being low to the ground lent a car a rakish, stylish look—something which would have appealed to Crosley. The wheels would have been shod with pneumatic rubber tires, anywhere from 2-1/4 to 6-1/2 inches wide. The heavier the car, the wider were the tires required— and the wider the tires, the smoother the ride.

The body would have been wood, perhaps reinforced with steel. Cost and the conventions of carriage makers still ruled in those days, and it was not until after 1912 that a major shift to steel auto bodies began. As for the style, it could have been a touring car or a runabout (roadster). Crosley's frame was large enough to support a touring car body, but as a roadster it would have been faster. Touring cars outsold other body styles, but a runabout may have appealed more to Crosley's aesthetic sense. He wrote of being taken with the $500 Ford Model N, which he saw for the first time in 1905 or 1906. Although it was a four-cylinder car, the Model N had all sorts of sporty appeal. It was a two-seater, with a boat-tail rear deck. It was lower to the ground than many cars (while still providing over a foot of ground-clearance) and the body was composed mainly of gentle curves. It could do 45 miles per hour.

Some roadsters included a detachable tonneau for rear seating, and Crosley could have gone with that sort of design.

Runabout or tourer, the Marathon Six probably had a top, considering the climate of the region and Crosley's later work in designing auto tops and side- and back-curtains. (He patented several designs.) The top could be supplied with the body—which probably was readymade. A custom-built body for the Marathon Six would have cost hundreds of dollars. An off-the-shelf body might cost $100 to $150; Henry Ford bought wooden bodies for his first Model A at $68 apiece, for 650 units. Because this was to be an economical car, the savings could have been important enough for Crosley to take that route. Custom or stock, a car body normally came painted, and upholstered with anything from cotton cord to leather to silk.

To modern eyes, the body would look like other car bodies of the era, with mostly angular lines broken by long curves. It would have had an extra-long hood to accommodate the engine, two seats in the front passenger compartment, and (in the case of a tourer) a larger area behind that for a bench seat with room for three or more. Mud guards of varnished leather or patent leather would rise over the wheels. (Perhaps these inspired the canvas fenders hung on the Crosley's WWII answer to the Jeep, the CT-3 "Pup.") Laminated wood or enameled metal mud guards were also available, at higher cost. Running boards would have eased entry for driver and passengers.

Considering Crosley's affection for the Ford Model N, the Marathon Six may have had a similar look as a roadster. He may have gone for a lower-slung look, though—in which case the Marathon Six would have resembled the famous Stutz Bearcat (still half a decade in the future). As a touring car, it might have looked a lot like Ford's Model K.

The body itself would follow the seating. Wider in the back than the front for a touring car, the body extended beyond the frame at the rear. There would be mild curves at the back corners, as illustrated by the standard body here. Elaborate curves and sculpting along the top and all edges of the body could have been added as "styling." Another styling decision would have been whether to put doors on the passenger compartment, or leave it open. Decorative brass trim on the body might add to its attractiveness, as could the shape of the mudguards and the angle of the steering wheel.

A window and frame, and perhaps dash gauges, would round out the body. If included, headlamps of the acetylene type probably were hung on extension brackets connected to the engine cowling.

A six-cylinder engine could be had for not much more than $200 from any of several manufacturers then engaged in building gasoline engines for stationary or motor vehicle use. The norm in 1907 was a vertical, in-line design. Depending on the bore and stroke, six-cylinder engines were commonly rated at 40 to 60 horsepower. A car of the size of the Marathon Six with that much power could easily reach a speed of 50 miles per hour.

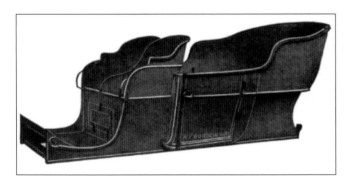

Example of readymade motorcar body, a large open touring car model offered by the H.F. Burbein Co. in 1906. *Banks collection*

Whatever its configuration, building the Marathon Six seems to have burned cash the way a V-12 burns gasoline—fast and in big gulps. By summer's end, after showing the car and collecting a half-dozen advance orders, Crosley was out of money. Maybe the young automaker miscalculated his development costs. Then, too, it could be that his backers were investing in stages and got cold feet when it came time for production—just when a nationwide financial downturn struck.

What became known as the Panic of 1907 hit the country in October. After a series of bank failures across the nation, the stock market faltered. Or maybe it was the other way around. Either way, there were runs on banks and other unpleasant events—not unlike those of a century later. Investors everywhere lost or held more tightly to money they might otherwise have invested in startups like the Marathon Six Automobile Company.

Over the next few months J.P. Morgan organized a strategy to keep America's economy from stalling. Judicious bailouts jump-started the banking system. But there was to be no bailout for Crosley's venture. The men with the money shook their heads and investment capital simply, as Crosley put it, "dried up."

And that was as far as it went—or so Crosley wanted his chroniclers to believe. Two decades later, he presented this tale as a mawkish melodrama of loss and woe. In an interview with *Radio Broadcast* magazine, he summed up the Marathon Six experience with, "I think that failure was the greatest disappointment in my life. I have never counted on anything so surely and taken a reverse to heart the way I mourned that automobile disaster."

Poor Powel…but it wasn't that way at all. The Marathon Six still had plenty of miles left on it.

(Note: Due to confusion involving the fact that the Lexington Motor Car Company coincidentally moved from Lexington, Kentucky, to Connersville in 1910, a few sources maintain that Crosley sold the design of the Marathon Six to Lexington. As you will see, he did not. Being an assembled car, there wasn't much of a design to sell, in any event.)

The story handed out after Powel Crosley, Jr., became a celebrity in the 1920s said that he wrote off the Marathon Six, salved his hurt feelings and slunk away to Indianapolis to seek his fortune. As it really happened, he did not write off the Marathon Six, but he did go to work at Carl Graham Fisher's Indianapolis auto dealership for a few months, until he broke his arm cranking a car.

Back at home toward the end of 1908, as the story continued, Crosley whiled away the time as he recovered. But that wasn't quite true, either. No one with Crosley's energy would have sat idle. He had ideas, and drive. He had a prototype automobile, a marketing plan and proven powers of persuasion. As far as Crosley was concerned (and despite what he said later), the game was far from over. All he needed was money….

Confident that he could find new investors in an economy that was almost back to normal—he had, after all, done it before—Crosley dusted off the Marathon Six and went looking for financiers. He made inquiries here and there among his contacts. He may or may not have approached former backers, but by the beginning of 1909 he had lined up serious financing. Impressed by the Marathon Six—by the fact that Crosley had a real automobile that he himself had assembled—six men were willing to put up a total of $30,000 to back a new Crosley company in Cincinnati. According to *Automotive Industries* magazine, the company's intent was to build a six-cylinder car.

Articles of incorporation for the Marathon Motor Car Company were filed in Ohio on February 16, 1909. Powel Crosley, Jr., was named president. The other officers were: Clifford Garvey, vice-president; John Rahn, Jr., second vice-president; Ralph Holterhoff, secretary; and Frank H. Simpson, treasurer. Two more investors showed up on the company's paperwork: C.L. La Boiteaux and William H. Carpenter.

Here was a group of well-established and affluent Cincinnatians who represented a cross-section of the city's business activities. La Boiteaux was a major paperboard manufacturer. Garvey had a number of interests and would become vice-president of Cincinnati's Trailmobile at its founding in 1916. Frank Simpson was a realtor and developer in Crosley's home town of College Hill. Rahn owned a thriving machine-tool company. Holterhoff was a life insurance executive who had attended the University of Cincinnati with Powel Crosley, Jr. And William H. Carpenter was Rahn's business partner.

With this revitalization, Powel Crosley, Jr. was back to work and drawing a salary. The office and factory of the Marathon Motor Car Company were located at 2935-41 Spring Grove Avenue (a few blocks from Crosley's future radio enterprise). Of note is the fact that the new company's building was part of a complex that housed John Rahn's huge machine tool manufactory, the Rahn-Larmon Company. This gave Crosley not only factory space but also machine tools, a pool of skilled workers and more. Now Powel Crosley had everything he needed to refine the Marathon and get it into production.

The only catch was that Crosley wouldn't have had everything his way as he did in Connersville. His investors were all local men. Rahn was on-site every day, where he could monitor Crosley's progress closely. Stubborn and independent, Crosley would have found having to answer to his investors annoying at the very least.

Was it annoying enough to make him leave town? Three months after the Marathon Motor Car Company got going, Crosley did exactly that. He went to Indianapolis and in the space of six months worked for the National Motor Vehicle Company, the Parry Automobile Company and an automotive trade journal. Each job involved a mixture of sales, marketing and advertising. While there, he spent a lot of time at the Indianapolis Motor Speedway, cultivating acquaintances among auto manufacturers, racing drivers, engineers and designers. (He did not, as he sometimes liked to let people think, drive in any races.)

Crosley later spoke of his time in Indianapolis as a time of learning. His purpose, he said later, was to learn everything he could about the automobile business. He certainly would have learned a lot, but what about the Marathon Motor Car Company? It was still in business. Was it possible that Crosley convinced his partners that his absence was in the interest of research?

Considering what happened following his sojourn to Indy, it's more likely that there had been a split between Crosley and Marathon.

After his time in Indianapolis, Crosley claimed, he took a job with the Inter-State Automobile Company in Muncie, Indiana. But here again he omitted some of the facts in order to shape the Crosley legend as he wanted it told. In truth, Powel Crosley, Jr., was back in Cincinnati by the end of 1909; and he did not rejoin the Marathon Motor Car Company. He went to work for a competing automaker. In coverage of the Cincinnati Automobile Show in its March 3, 1910, issue, *The Automobile* magazine reported: "Powel Crosley, of the Haberer Company, which makes the Cino, booked an agency in Indianapolis which has contracted for 25 cars."

This job—perhaps to Crosley just another learning experience—lasted six months. In September, 1910, a news item in *Motor Age* headed "Crosley Starts Company" reported: "Powel Crosley, Jr., formerly of National

Motor Vehicle Co., Indianapolis, has organized the Central Motor Sales Co. and opened offices and salesrooms at 305 East Main Street. Muncie, Ind. This concern will act as distributor for the Inter-State in northern Indiana and will add several lower-priced cars to fill out a complete line."

Now he was running a new-car dealership, selling Inter-State and other makes. It was from this he spun the tale of working for Inter-State. Inter-State was owned in part by his cousin's husband, the wealthy Edmund Ball, who may have arranged Crosley's dealership. Crosley stayed with the business through part of 1911 and then returned to Cincinnati for good. The most compelling reason for this had to be the fact that he was now married and a father, and his family was in Cincinnati. He may or may not have received a settlement when he gave up the dealership.

Interestingly, the revival of the Marathon, his work for Haberer and the new car dealership show up nowhere in Crosley's reminiscences. What really happened with Crosley and these companies? Did they want him to go in a direction he didn't want to go—or vice-versa? Was he forced out, or did he walk out? With everyone involved now long-gone, the answers to those questions may never be known.

What is known is that Crosley was hard at work on another six-cylinder car during 1912. This one was called the Hermes. Despite striking out twice with the Marathon and failing or quitting several times in auto sales, Powel Crosley, Jr., was not giving up on the automobile.

His new business was the Hermes Motor Car Company, incorporated in December 1912. According to the January 6, 1913, issue of *Industrial World*, the Hermes plant would be located in the Cincinnati industrial suburb of Cumminsville. Long-range plans for the company were to produce automobiles, trucks and accessories.

The effort was headed by Albert Kleybolte, son of Crosley's former employer. Powel Crosley, Jr., was named second among the investors, followed by Charles Eisen, Walter H. Aiken and John C. Rogers. Rogers was an attorney and an associate of Powel Crosley's father. Aiken was Crosley's father-in-law. Charles Eisen headed a huge chocolate company that employed 400. (Eisen was involved with setting up a concern called the Herman Motor Company at the same time. The similarity of company names is suggestive, but no link has been found between Crosley and the Herman Motor Company.)

Capital was set at $30,000, with a vague promise that funding would be increased to $100,000 or $200,000 once the company got on a firm footing. Kleybolte doesn't show up anywhere else in the automotive world, so there is a good possibility that Crosley was the idea man. But the fact that he wasn't in charge may well have irked Crosley. After all, he was the auto designer. He had the experience.

Just weeks after Hermes' incorporation *The Automobile* announced, "The Hermes Motor Company Cincinnati, O., has built its first car. It will be sold for $1,700." It appears that most of the work on the Hermes had taken place during 1912.

We know a little more about what went into the Hermes than the Marathon Six. The car's full name was the Hermes 6-50. With a 124-inch wheelbase, it was a large car and needed a big engine. That engine was made by the Beaver Manufacturing Company of Milwaukee, and the Hermes borrowed its specifications for its name. The 6-50 was an inline six-cylinder power plant that produced 50 horsepower (45 bhp). If not the exact model Beaver engine used in the Hermes 6-50, the accompanying image is very much like it.

By now, metal bodies were in vogue, and the Hermes probably had a steel body, as well as steel mudguards and running boards. The wheelbase would have accommodated an even larger touring car body than could the Marathon Six, with lots of leg room and perhaps a trunk in addition to two rows of seats.

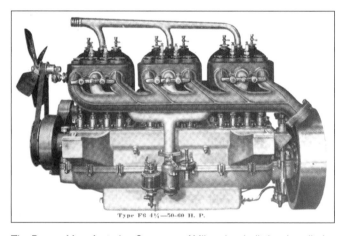

The Beaver Manufacturing Company of Milwaukee built the six-cylinder engine used in the Hermes Motor Car. It was an L-head, configured with three banks of two cast-iron cylinders bolted vertically to its crankcase. Displacement was 377 cubic inches (6.2 liters). Bore and stroke were 4 inches and 5 inches, respectively. It was a big six, and the Beaver was especially proud of the large crankshafts in its engines—one of its advertising slogans was "a crankshaft big as your wrist." It probably got 16 miles per gallon. *Banks collection*

Beginning a tradition that would mark most of Crosley's future consumer products, the Hermes had a couple of features to help it stand out from the ever-growing pack of competitors. It featured an electric starter, Charles Kettering's 1912 invention. The presence of a starter implies the Hermes had battery-powered headlights. It also had wire wheels, the spokes made of shorter and thicker wire than bicycle wheels. Short spokes meant smaller-diameter wheels—which would have given it an attractive, modern look. Next to cars with pressed steel or wooden wheels, the Hermes would have glittered as it rolled down Cincinnati's streets.

Unfortunately, the "$100,000 or $200,000" in new capital did not materialize after the Hermes prototype was completed. In March 1913, Crosley and Kleybolte were meeting with potential investors in Hamilton, Ohio, hoping to raise another $50,000 immediately. As an inducement, they offered to move the Hermes factory to Hamilton. But no new money was forthcoming and the Hermes Motor Car Company was finished.

It didn't help that a recession was on. Crosley couldn't have failed to notice the irony in that, and his frustration must have been intense.

Crosley's former company wasn't quite finished. The Marathon Motor Car Company shows up on lists of active corporations at this time, but with new owners.

And trade journal reports suggest that it switched to automobile sales rather than manufacturing. In fact, the Marathon Motor Car Company was in the process of building new showrooms.

Crosley took a job selling advertising for a Cincinnati agency and worked at freelance copywriting jobs on the side. With the Hermes Motor Car Company out of his life, he shifted his focus to yet another car. This time it was a cyclecar. Cyclecars were small, very light cars built for one or two passengers. They weighed less than a thousand pounds and were usually powered by motorcycle engines and rode on bicycle wheels. Some said they were more motorcycles than cars; others said they were halfway between motorcycles and cars. Their low cost (an average of $500) and low operating expense made them very attractive to people who couldn't afford a normal-sized automobile.

The most distinctive features of the mini-mobiles were a short wheelbase, typically 100 inches, and a particularly narrow track, 36 inches. A low center of gravity made them fairly maneuverable and less likely to tip over on turns. They were wildly popular—especially among the scores of manufacturers and would-be manufacturers popping up around the country. (In the 21st Century, various government agencies would have banned them from public roads and probably prevented their sale.)

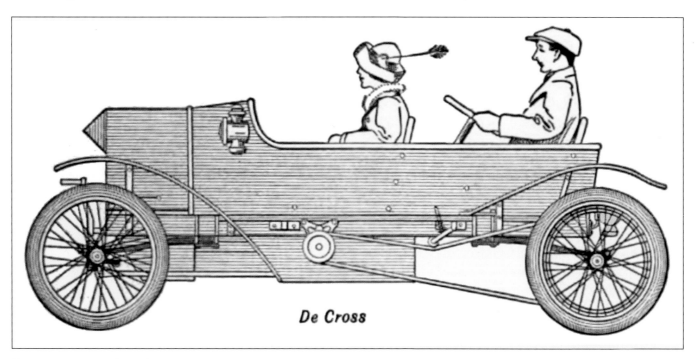

De Cross

This sketch of the DeCross Cyclecar appeared in cyclecar publications and a book in 1913. It is a clear representation of Crosley's eye-catching approach to design. The driver sat behind and above the passenger. The body was wood, and as with other cyclecars the DeCross rolled on lightweight bicycle wheels, the axles connected to the body with quarter-elliptic leaf springs. Headlamps, probably magneto-powered, were mounted on the sides. The fenders or mudshields were wood or metal. *Banks collection*

Seen from above, another cyclecar of a similar design gives an idea of just how narrow the DeCross was. Few cyclecar builders offered interiors as opulent as this one, fitted out with padded leather. *Banks collection*

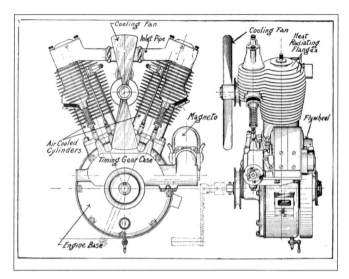

Engineering diagram for the Spacke 9-13 De-Luxe cyclecar engine. The model was so-named because it developed 9 brake horsepower and 13 shaft horsepower. Today it would be called a "V-twin." The engine was crank-started and included a belt-driven fan to supplement natural airflow. Displacement was 12.7 cubic inches (208 cc). *Banks collection*

Powel Crosley's cyclecar was named the DeCross, perhaps a combination of Crosley's name with that of his backer, Godfrey Doeller. Doeller was a civil engineer from Hamilton, Ohio, who had attended the University of Cincinnati with the Crosley brothers and was a fellow member of Phi Delta Theta. After working on the little car for some months, the two got around to incorporating the DeCross Cyclecar Company on October 16, 1913. (There is evidence that the DeCross was taken for test drives in July of that year.) It was sometimes referred to as the DeCross Cy-Car Company.

As can be seen in the illustration, the DeCross had a blocky wood body with mudguards front and rear. Sidelamps lit the forward view; they may have been magneto-powered. Like the Hermes, the DeCross cyclecar had features that made it decidedly different from the competition. The most obvious departure was that the passenger did not sit next to or behind the driver, but rather in front of the driver.

The DeCross included another element that would become a Crosley marketing trademark: low cost. It was built, as he would say of future Crosley products, "for the masses and not the classes." The philosophy was not unlike that which Henry Ford expressed for the Model T: to provide a quality product at a low price.

The DeCross was powered by a two-cylinder, air-cooled engine like that shown here, manufactured by the Spacke Machine and Tool Company of Indianapolis. (A Spacke engine also powered a cyclecar that Spacke built for Sears to sell under its own name.)

A motorcycle-style belt drive turned one of the rear wheels, and a primitive mechanical clutch was used to disengage the belt from the drive pulley. Top speed was probably 40 to 45 mph. The axles were mounted directly to four quarter-elliptic springs, and fat tires helped smooth the ride and ease braking. Cyclecar braking was

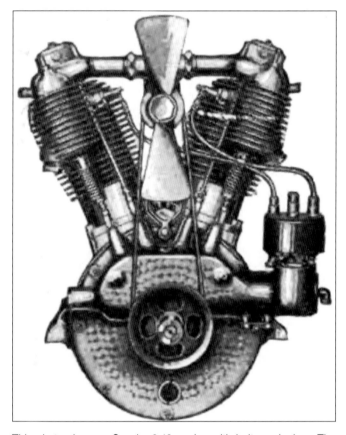

This photo shows a Spacke 9-13 engine with belts and wires. The air-cooled power plant propelled the DeCross to 40-50 mph. *Banks collection*

accomplished by a mechanism that moved the rear axle against fixed brake shoes.

Crosley took the DeCross out frequently, and made the 70-mile roundtrip to Hamilton and back more than once. For publicity, he entered the DeCross in an event called the Around-Lake-Michigan reliability contest set for October 1913. The endurance run would follow the entire shoreline of Lake Michigan, and was the first sanctioned cyclecar event held in the United States. (The annual event was actually for automobiles of all kinds, but a special cyclecar division was established for 1913.)

The Michigan tour would have been a one-week event but it was cancelled in late summer. A Chicago-to-Indianapolis "sociability run" limited to cyclecars replaced it. The DeCross was not listed among the run's winners.

Powel Crosley still retained an interest in cyclecars. When the Cyclecar Association of America was formed in April 1914, Crosley was a founding member. He may also have joined the competing Cyclecar Manufacturers National Association. Nothing more of was heard of the DeCross, though. As Crosley explained matters, the DeCross failed because (again) there was no money for production.

In any event, the industry was so top-heavy with manufacturers that few sold more than a handful of cars. In addition, the price of full-size cars (at least light, full-size cars) was coming down. For example, Ford lowered the price of its Model T to $550 in 1913. This cut sharply into the cyclecar market.

After seven years of trying, Powel Crosley, Jr., had chalked up four automobile manufacturing companies and four failures.

Powel Crosley, Jr., as a young man. *Banks collection*

CHAPTER 2

1915-1934: Huckster and Inventor

Powel Crosley scraped by as a freelance advertising copywriter over the next year. From time to time he sold printing and advertising novelties. It was a desultory living. Years later he told one interviewer that his income was so low that buying a bottle of wine when he took his wife out for dinner was a rare event.

"Poor Powel," again? It was certainly in keeping with the rags-to-riches theme he tried to weave into his personal legend.

Poor or not, in the course of his advertising work he met a Dayton businessman named Ira J. Cooper. Among other activities Cooper manufactured recapped tires. In 1915, Cooper and several partners established a mail-order automobile accessories business called the White Manufacturing Company in Cincinnati. White Manufacturing's products included a gasoline additive called "Gaso-Tonic," a carryover from a previous Cooper effort. The additive promised to clean out engines and increase mileage. Just add an ounce to every five gallons of gasoline.

Independent tests by consumer agencies in three states eventually revealed that Gaso-Tonic was nothing more than low-octane gasoline with a green coloring agent. Cooper was stuck with thousands of bottles of the stuff and was desperate to sell them. He asked Crosley to develop an advertising campaign to spur sales. Crosley came up with press releases, magazine ads and newspaper classifieds that soon had the quart bottles of green gasoline racing out of the warehouse. Crosley's catchy ads called it "the Mystery of Motordom" and promised that Gaso-Tonic would increase gas mileage as much as 25, 40 and even 50 percent. It would remove carbon from any engine and perform other unlikely miracles. Bogus testimonials praised it. Motorists could make big money selling it, too—*guaranteed!* It sold well for a couple years—until the truth got out or readers tired of

the advertising. Crosley either didn't realize what this actually was, or felt no sense of guilt because he was distanced from the source by being the ad copywriter.

Cooper was impressed, and asked Crosley to come up with ideas for more products. Crosley showed Cooper a safety device he'd designed and used on his own Model T Ford. The invention, which Crosley called the "Litl Sho-Fur," helped steer the car in an emergency. The idea was that if a Model T hit a bump or pothole hard enough to jerk the steering wheel out of the driver's hands, the gadget would pull the front wheels back to a straight track. A leaf spring mounted sideways between

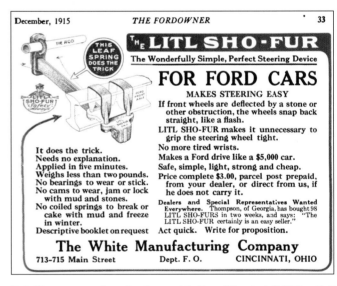

Detail from a magazine advertisement for Powel Crosley's "Litl Sho-Fur" safety mechanism for Model T Fords. If a Model T equipped with this device hit a bump or chuckhole hard enough to yank the steering wheel from the driver's hands, the leaf spring forced the wheels back onto a straight path. It was one of Crosley's top-selling products when he was in the auto accessories business, and popular enough that Sears added it to its own auto accessories catalog. Powel Crosley, Jr., was awarded U.S. Patent number 1,214,651 for the steering attachment. *Banks Collection*

Ira J. Cooper, who gave Powel Crosley, Jr., his start in the automobile accessories business—Crosley's first real success. Cooper hired Crosley to help him market products through his White Manufacturing Company, and then backed some of Crosley's automotive inventions. Together, the two formed the American Automobile Accessories Company. Crosley later bought out Cooper, who was already in the tire and rubber business, and went on to become a major player in the industry with the Cooper Tire & Rubber Company. It is arguable that, without Cooper, Powel Crosley, Jr., might not have amassed the money needed to launch his fledgling radio business in 1921—and thus may never have had enough money to launch the Crosley automobile. *Courtesy of the Cooper Tire & Rubber Company*

the front axle and tie rod did the trick. Cooper agreed to back the Litl Sho-Fur for production, and Crosley applied for a patent. By the end of 1915 the Litl Sho-Fur was selling in auto magazines, *Popular Mechanics* and even the *Fordowner* magazine at three dollars a pop. And Crosley was in for a fifty-percent share of the profits.

On a roll, Crosley presented to Cooper a gadget he called the "Little Fiend." Attach it to your carburetor, and your engine could "burn free air" rather than gasoline. They put it on the market. Later on, Crosley would develop the "Booster auxiliary water carburetor" that, according to his ads, would make autos burn water. (Where are these wonders today?)

The young inventor's next idea—a protective liner for tires—was prompted by a problem facing Cooper in his tire retreading business. The operation accumulated thousands of tire carcasses so worn that they couldn't be recapped. Disposing of them was difficult. Cooper challenged Crosley to find a way to put those old tires to use.

Crosley's response was to use this problem to solve another problem: the high incidence of flat tires that plagued motorists. Automobile tires of the day were made of thin rubber and fabric. They were easily punctured and wore out after only a few thousand miles. The solution was to turn multiple layers of the old fabric-and-rubber material into tire liners. Make liners to match popular tire sizes, add a special kind of glue to bond them to the insides of customers' tires and sell the product for a tenth of the price of a new tire. Cooper liked the idea and gave Crosley the go-ahead to market it.

As already demonstrated, Crosley had a predilection for coming up with catchy names. He dubbed this creation "Insyde Tyres," because that's where the liners went and the British spelling would catch attention. The summer of 1916 saw ads for Insyde Tyres and the Little Fiend appearing in automobile magazines and in hundreds of newspapers across the country. White Manufacturing raked it in while customers got fewer flats and more miles out of their tires. And Powel Crosley, Jr., earned another patent.

Crosley and Cooper soon incorporated a partnership called the American Automobile Accessories Company to market Insyde Tyres and Crosley's other ideas, independent of Cooper's partners in White Manufacturing. The new company sometimes went by "Americo," "American Accessories" or "the 3A Co." (Yet another independent operation was set up to sell Gaso-Tonic.)

As he worked his way to success, Crosley designed another six-cylinder car. But there was no money. He was doing well, but he didn't have the hundred thousand dollars (or more) it now would take to launch a car and get it into production. So he set aside the new car design and concentrated on expanding the auto accessories business.

In 1917 he bought out Cooper for $1,500. (Cooper had other, more lucrative interests. The now-famous Cooper Tire & Rubber Company was one of them.) Crosley's product line included the Litl Sho-Fur, the Little Fiend, Insyde Tyres and a windshield draft eliminator to make Model Ts more comfortable in winter. Soon enough, the company was selling an entire catalog of automobile merchandise—everything from car tops

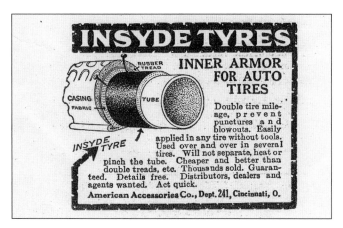

Powel Crosley's second successful idea was Insyde Tyres. This tire-shaped liner for automobile tires protected inner tubes from road hazards, and allowed cars to continue running on seriously worn tires. The tire-liner later was sold mail-order by Sears, and Crosley had an extensive program in which he enlisted buyers of the product to sell it for him. *Banks Collection*

Powel Crosley knew that motorists were keen for any product that would make their cars use less gasoline. So, in addition to gadgets that were supposed to allow cars to run on air and water, he came out with a gasoline fortifier called "Kick." It offered everything that Gaso-Tonic promised, and delivered about as much. Still, many motorists were certain that there had to be a way to get more miles out of a gallon of gas—an easy, simple way. This was why Gaso-Tonic, Kick and similar gasoline additives sold so well. If these miracles were peddled by anonymous companies with no street addresses, well that just had to be because the oil companies wouldn't want them to be sold in stores, lest they sell less gasoline. *Banks Collection*

Crosley's American Automobile Accessories Company (aka "Americo") offered batteries, tires, tools, spark plugs, tops, seats and even entire bodies for automobiles. Specialties included such Crosley inventions as the Litl Sho-Fur, Insyde Tyres, a miracle gasoline additive called "Kick," wash-and-wax products, blowout patches, flag holders and other decorative items, and just about anything else an auto enthusiast could want. Crosley liked to dream up items for the Ford Model T, "because there are so many of them." Customers were invited to become freelance Americo representatives and sell from the catalog. *Banks Collection*

and tires to car wax, spark plugs and tools. A number of specialized items were offered for the Ford Model T. Much of what the company sold—rubber goods in particular—was manufactured at a factory in Cincinnati's Northside neighborhood, a block off Hamilton Avenue.

Interestingly, Crosley also sold a "gasoline fortifier" that he called "Kick," for which he used the same ads that were so effective in moving Gaso-Tonic. Might it have been that Kick was simply a clever repackaging of Gaso-Tonic? Judging from the periods during which the two products were advertised, Kick seems to have hit the market just as Gaso-Tonic was fading.

A consistent theme in advertising for the White Manufacturing Company had been offering customers the opportunity to make money with White products. Anyone who responded to ads was given a schedule of "confidential discount prices for agents." These special prices weren't really special at all; they were a psychological device intended to encourage potential customers to buy, letting them think they were getting a price no one else could get. In reality, every customer paid the "agent" prices. Crosley expanded this idea to cover everything in the American Automobile Accessories catalog.

As the United States entered the war in Europe, Powel Crosley managed to become a military supplier. (At the age of 31 and the father of two children, he wasn't a candidate for the draft.) He also learned quite a bit about military procurement. This would be useful during the next war. His brother, Lewis, was already in the Army Corps of Engineers when World War I broke out, and spent a good deal of time in France handling construction as well as property disposal and sales. After Lewis returned from Europe, he joined Powel's company. A degreed civil engineer with superior organizational and planning skills, Lewis took over daily operations, while Powel focused on marketing and exploring new avenues of business. The brothers created a division called "the Crosley Manufacturing Company" and experimented with building phonographs and other non-automotive products. Crosley fine-tuned his pitches and sold several Americo products wholesale to Sears, the mail-order giant. Among them were the Litl Sho-Fur and Insyde Tyres. Within a couple of years he was making quite a bit of money, but still not enough to put an automobile into production.

Then Crosley discovered radio. As has often been told, he more or less backed into the field. In 1921 his son had asked him for one of the radio receivers that were just then hitting the market. (They were banned during the war.) Crosley thought radio receivers were overpriced and decided that he and his son could build one themselves for less. He bought the necessary parts, learned about radio and soon was producing radio components and receivers at a fraction of what other manufacturers charged. Like the DeCross, Crosley radios were built "for the masses, not the classes." In 1922 he threw in something extra. To give his customers a reason to buy radio sets, he started a radio station, WLW in Cincinnati.

Crosley established the Crosley Radio Corporation to build radios. (The American Automobile Accessories company remained in operation.) Radio sales doubled, then doubled again as more broadcasters went on the air. In less than three years, Crosley's new company was the world's largest radio manufacturer, thanks to low prices and aggressive marketing—and the built-in "extra" of WLW.

Crosley periodically increased the station's broadcast

Powel Crosley, Jr., discovered radio almost by accident when his son asked for a set after he'd seen one at a friend's home. Crosley knew receivers could be built for far less than retailers were selling them and after building a set with his son, Powel, III, he began manufacturing and marketing both radio parts and complete receiving sets. His new company, the Crosley Radio Corporation, quickly became the largest manufacturer of radios in the world. Crosley radios were sold on every continent, all manufactured in and shipped from Cincinnati, Ohio, USA. *Banks Collection*

power in order to maintain the low production cost of his receivers by reducing the number of components each set required. As Crosley often said of WLW, "The more power I put into it, the cheaper I can build radios."

With the manufacture and marketing of Crosley radios, Powel Crosley, Jr., perfected a specific approach to consumer products. Crosley radios cost less than competing brands. Buyers would get something extra, like free headphones. And most Crosley products would be different. They would stand out from the crowd of competing products by virtue of features or appearance, or both. These philosophies would carry through to the

Founded to give people a reason to buy radios, as well as to advertise them, Powel Crosley's broadcasting station, WLW, could be heard across much of North America from its beginnings. Crosley increased the station's power periodically, in order to boost advertising and enable Crosley Radio Corporation to continue manufacturing low-cost receivers. Throughout most of the 1930s WLW was the most powerful commercial station in the world and played an important role in America's war effort with high-power propaganda broadcasts beyond the U.S. This Arlington St. building still stands. *Banks Collection*

Powel Crosley, Jr., poses with one of his "Moonbeam" series airplanes. Crosley Aircraft built five biplanes and monoplanes near Cincinnati between 1929 and 1932, incorporating many innovative features. The company never got into the production of aircraft. All but one of the Moonbeams was destroyed in a hangar fire in 1935. Today, the Ford Motor Company's Sharonville transmission plant occupies the former site of Crosley's airport. The only surviving Moonbeam is on display at the Kentucky Museum of Aviation at Lexington International Airport. *Banks Collection*

design and marketing of the Crosley automobile.

The first half of the 1930s found Crosley too busily occupied to consider automobile manufacturing. The closest he came was introducing the world's second automobile radio, the "Roamio," in 1931. (Motorola beat him to market by weeks.) Throughout the late 1920s and most of the 1930s he was busy building mansions in Cincinnati and Florida, plus getaways in Indiana, Canada, South Carolina and the Caribbean. He spent weeks at a time hunting and fishing.

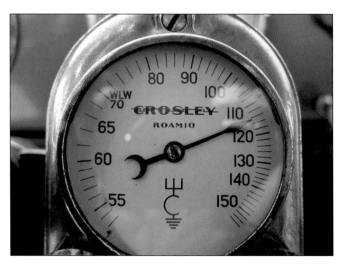

A Crosley Roamio automobile radio installed in a 1946 Crosley CC pickup truck. The truck is shown in the next photo. The control head, with dial, plus tuning and volume controls, is mounted on a bracket connected to the pickup's steering column. Note the "WLW" on the dial; Powel Crosley, Jr., used one product to advertise another as often as possible. Owner Bill Angert installed the aftermarket product. Not incidentally the pickup truck has its original COBRA engine. *Photo by Bill Angert*

Here's how the Roamio looked to the driver of the pickup truck in which it is installed. Powel Crosley would have said, "It is entirely safe. It can be tuned in and adjusted without taking a hand off the wheel!" The "guts" are under the dash, and the existing speaker grill (half of which can be seen at the far right) accommodated the speaker. *Photo by Bill Angert*

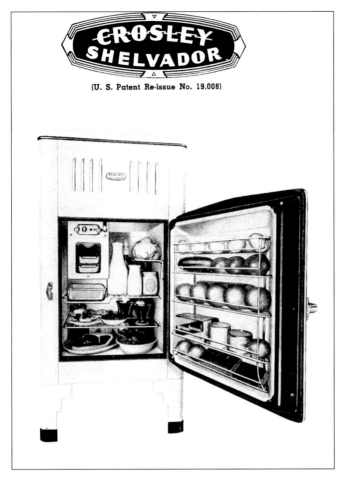

Before the Crosley Shelvador, refrigerators had no shelves in their doors. After Crosley Radio bought the patent rights, only Crosley had shelves in refrigerator doors. *Banks Collection*

Newspapers via radio—that's what the Crosley READO would have brought to America's living rooms. *Banks Collection*

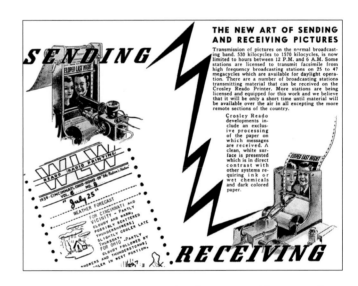

An aviation enthusiast, Crosley owned a number of airplanes from the 1920s through the 1950s, although he wasn't licensed to fly. Instead, he hired a veteran pilot to take him where he wanted to go. He bought airplanes, seaplanes and yachts, often getting rid of a new one almost as soon as it was broken in. For a brief time in the 1920s he was an investor in an airline and in an aircraft manufacturing company, Metal Aircraft Corporation.

In 1929 Crosley got into aircraft building on his own with Crosley Aircraft. He developed an airport on 193 acres outside Cincinnati, where he built a huge factory/hangar. The company's prototype biplanes and monoplanes were well-received, and Crosley Aircraft engineers generated several patents. But no aircraft went into regular production. At the same time, Crosley was a dealer for the Pitcairn autogyro. After turning out just five airplanes, Crosley shut down the undertaking and used the field as his private airport. All told, the aviation venture cost Crosley $300,000. (One wonders: why airplanes and not automobiles?)

Clear of the aircraft business, Powel Crosley, Jr., returned his attention to radio. In 1934 WLW became the world's most powerful commercial radio station when a new, experimental transmitter sent out WLW's signal at 500,000 watts—and sometimes higher. Other stations remained limited to 50,000 watts, a situation that eventually would cause political problems for Crosley, a staunch Republican.

Also in 1934, Crosley took a controlling interest in the Cincinnati Reds baseball team. A Reds fan since childhood, this was almost a dream-come-true for the radio magnate. The move ostensibly was to keep the

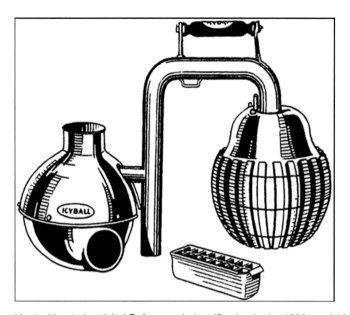

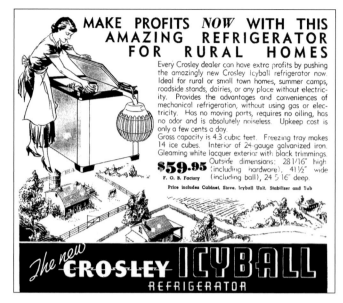

Heat without electricity! Before rural electrification in the 1930s and 1940s, people outside of cities and towns had no way to refrigerate foods and medicines. The Crosley Icyball changed that. It made cold from heat. "Charged" by heating one end over a kerosene burner once a day, the Icyball could refrigerate several cubic feet for 24 hours, and even make ice. *Banks Collection*

Reds from moving from Cincinnati, but Crosley enjoyed involvement with the team. He ordered the upgrading of the team's park, Redland Field, and soon afterward renamed it "Crosley Field."

Crosley Aircraft and the ownership of the Cincinnati Reds were private ventures on Powel Crosley's part, not related to the Crosley Radio Corporation, which had gone public in 1928. For its part, the company prospered while the founder pursued other interests. It continued to diversify, expanding into home appliances of all sorts, most notably refrigerators. In that field the company scored a monopoly by buying the patent rights to the idea of building shelves in refrigerator doors. (Crosley named the new refrigerator the "Shelvador.") Crosley helped found NBC. And he turned out oddball products, among them a home radio/FAX machine that he hoped would replace printed newspapers, and the Icyball, a refrigerator that operated without electricity, powered by heat from a kerosene burner. There was also a hair-growing machine called the "Xervac." Like Gaso-Tonic, the Xervac would be proven to be so much hokum. The Federal Trade Commission apparently forced it off the market, even though Crosley himself swore that it helped him retain his hair.

And then, after all the experiments and toys, the expansions and acquisitions, Powel Crosley, Jr., decided it was time to build cars.

Like so many others before and since, Powel Crosley thought that he had discovered a way to restore his thinning hair. He tried to share his miracle device, the XERVAC, with other men— for a fee—but the Federal Trade Commission objected. *Banks Collection*

CHAPTER 3
1935-1940: The Car of Tomorrow

Aside from making him a civic hero, buying control of the Cincinnati Reds demanded considerable amounts of attention and cash from Crosley. And even with Lewis doing much of the heavy lifting at the Crosley Radio Corporation, Powel still had responsibilities there, especially after the company went public. He might take off a month at a time, but he still had work to do. As important as his automotive dream was, it seemed there was always something to take him away from the project.

But he was committed. And this time Powel Crosley would not have to find backers. Nor would he risk any of his personal fortune. The car would be built under the aegis of the Crosley Radio Corporation. Crosley created a special division for the car, dubbed the Crosley Radio Automotive Division, or CRAD. The prototype car that resulted also was called the CRAD, pending a more marketable name. Two Crosley Radio Corporation engineers were brought in to consult on the mechanical aspects: Sanford F. Clifton and L.C. Oswald, the latter as chief engineer.

Crosley's personal cars in those years were mostly Fords, with the occasional Lincoln—plus a big Deusenberg Beverly Berline (sedan) SJ designed by Gordon M. Buehrig. Roomy, powerful cars, all—but Crosley had for some time maintained an interest in small cars. Surprisingly, at 6 feet, 4 inches in height, he owned a tiny American Austin, a licensed version of the British Austin Seven design built in the United States. This miniature automobile was extremely popular car in England, and often called "the British Model T."

The American Austin was the smallest production car seen since the days of the cyclecar. Built on a 75-inch wheelbase with a 40-inch track, it was just ten feet long and not quite four-and-a-half feet wide. Styling was by designer Alexis de Sakhnoffsky.

The American Austin was powered by a 46-cubic-inch (747-cc) straight four-cylinder that produced 14 horsepower. Crosley used the Austin around his Sarasota, Florida, estate at the beginning of the 1930s and from the reports of his neighbors he enjoyed driving it,

even though getting into and out of the tiny car was a challenge for anyone his size.

One has to wonder whether, when Crosley rolled up his sleeves to work on the design of his automobile, the Austin influenced him. The midget auto matched his philosophy regarding products: it was different, cost less and offered something special. It had to be that the American Austin at least suggested to Crosley the idea of building a small car.

By 1935, when Crosley was able to set aside serious time for his pet project, the American Austin Car Company had gone bankrupt. In four years of production it sold about 20,000 units. The operation was taken over by an Austin employee named Roy S. Evans, who rechristened the car and company "American Bantam." Sakhnoffsky brightened up the design a bit, and Evans had his engineers make some mechanical improvements. The size was essentially the same, with a 75-inch wheelbase. However, while the front track was 40 inches, the rear track was wider at 42 inches. Production started in 1937.

The American Bantam was cute, and today it is a classic, but like the American Austin it did not sell well. About 3,500 were built that year, and 2,000 the next. Things continued downhill until 1941 when only 138 were built and the company ceased production. The reason: In Europe small cars were king. High gasoline prices, horsepower taxes and narrow lanes gave carbuyers plenty of motivation to choose small cars. In America, cheap gasoline and wide highways invited people to drive the biggest, fastest cars they could afford. In spite of all that, and despite the poor sales of the American Austin, here was Powel Crosley ready to build a small car. Still, there was the precedent of the famous "curved dash" Oldsmobile in 1903, which was a wildly successful small car in a time when nothing like it existed.

In addition to being small, or "light," as Crosley preferred to describe it, Crosley's auto would be different in several noticeable ways. The selling price would be

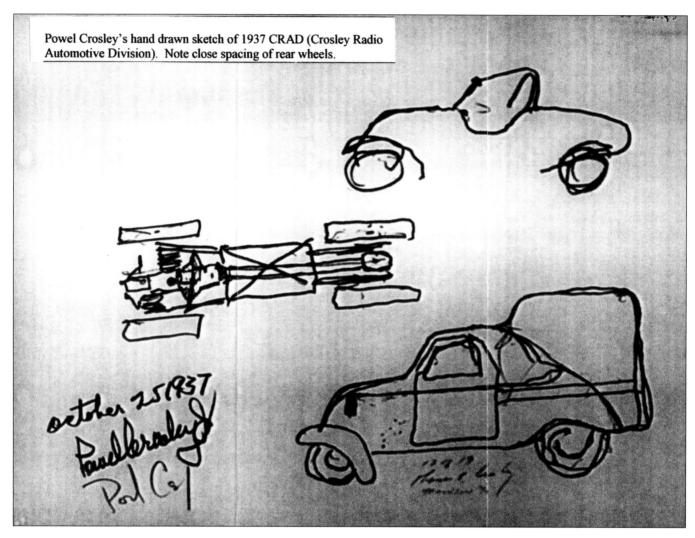

This rough sketch by Powel Crosley of his initial automobile design was drawn on a piece of corrugated cardboard (probably part of a Crosley radio shipping box). It clearly shows the narrow track of the rear wheels. Front fenders that were little more than cycle fenders, and engine-cowl-mounted headlights were additional distinctive features. The coupe featured a sloping rear end, a nod to streamlining. Crosley superimposed a covered truck bed over the car's rear. This was his idea for a panel-delivery style vehicle. He also sketched a jaunty two-seater runabout—of which nothing more was seen. *Banks Collection*

far below that of other American cars. And it would be a three-wheeler. *That* would get attention. The single wheel was to be in the rear, and it would propel the car. This meant saving money by eliminating a wheel, tire, universal joint and differential from the parts list. Depending on the body and chassis design it might save material in other ways. Crosley probably made up a long list of the benefits that a three-wheeled car would confer on its owner. It was his way to have a counter for any objection anyone might raise about his products.

The Crosley would have a two-cylinder engine, for economy. The engine would be air-cooled, perhaps simply to be different. Although the power such an engine developed wouldn't be anything like that of a four-cylinder, Crosley felt that a properly-made light car could

be peppy. And roomy enough for four adults, as long as they weren't too large. It would deliver all that was required of an automobile in a nation where most auto trips were made by one or two people in cars designed to carry six. "Why," Crosley would ask time and again, "would you take a battleship to cross a creek?"

The three-wheel configuration was abandoned early on. Crosley may have decided that it was unstable, or too radical to be taken seriously. Whatever his reasons, Crosley redesigned the chassis with its rear wheels set 18 inches apart. This approach still eliminated the need for a universal joint at the rear axle, using a ring-and-pinion gear to connect with the torque-tube driveshaft. Plus, it lent the car an exotic air. (Was the idea of mismatched front and rear tracks inspired by the American Bantam?)

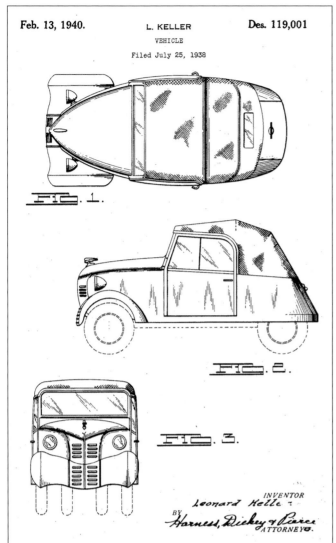

Feb. 13, 1940.   L. KELLER   Des. 119,001
VEHICLE
Filed July 25, 1938

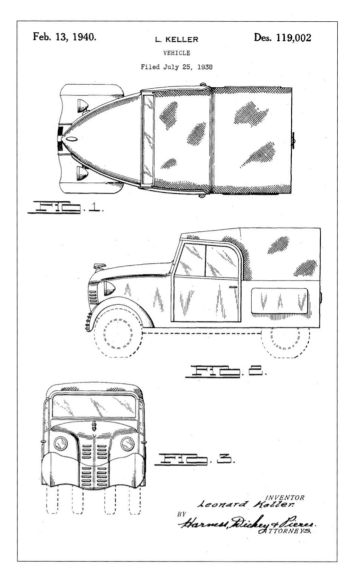

Feb. 13, 1940.   L. KELLER   Des. 119,002
VEHICLE
Filed July 25, 1938

Leonard Keller, a designer whose automotive portfolio included work for Graham-Paige, created this design for the Crosley coupe. He was an employee of the Murray Body Company of Detroit. Keller's design patent clearly shows the close-tracked rear wheels. Half-circle front fenders framed a high nose, although from above the front end that framed the pointed nose seemed square. With the 18-inch rear track, there was no need for rear fenders, nor a wheel well. The body's sides were faired into a narrow back end without even a token bumper. There was very little overhang beyond the wheels, front or rear. The cross-hatching of the top implies fabric, as do the lines of the supporting bows showing through. A small rear window is set into the fabric. *U.S. Trademark & Patent Office*

The design for the truck version of the Crosley used the same front end and doors as the Coupe, down to and including the curved upper-rear corners of the doors. Again, there were no bumpers. Behind the doors was a square pickup bed or box. The truck features fabric sides and top supported by a light internal framework of bows, perhaps a foreshadowing of the "covered wagon" model Crosley would produce beginning in 1941. The removable top begins at the windshield and extends to the rear of the truck—all in a one-piece construction. Hence, the design can be a covered truck or a pickup with the passenger compartment either covered or open. The rectangular construction on the side of the pickup bed may have been intended as a storage compartment for the top. *U.S. Trademark & Patent Office*

As Crosley first envisioned it, his car looked a lot like a Chevrolet coupe in profile, although lines similar to Chrysler's Airflow dominated the front end. Small, floating fenders stood out in front, while shallow wheel wells broke the rear lines. Crosley imagined several versions of the body to serve as pleasure and delivery vehicles.

The ultimate Crosley body design came from a draftsman-designer at the Murray Body Company of Detroit, named Leonard Keller. Murray would build the bodies for all pre-War Crosleys. The company had dealt with the Crosley Corporation in the past, turning out steel stampings for refrigerators. There were two designs: one a slope-backed coupe with a canvas top, the other a canvas-topped pickup truck. The patent ap-

The chassis for the CRAD was built as a one-off, for Crosley's use in what he referred to as "experiments." In this photo, Powel Crosley, Jr., is driving the bare chassis, with his grandson, Lew, as a passenger. In 1937, a body following Keller's design was fitted to the CRAD chassis. *Photo courtesy of the Crosley Automobile Club*

plications were filed on July 25, 1938, but the design was developed from Crosley's preliminary sketch well before that date.

As illustrated in the design patent drawings, the car and truck shared front ends and doors, and the rear tread of each was decidedly smaller than the front. Half-circle fenders framed a high, pointed nose, although from above the front end appeared to be square. The sides were faired into a narrow, fenderless rear end. There was very little overhang, front or rear. The patent applications were filed on July 25, 1938, but the design was developed from Crosley's preliminary sketch well before that.

There has been speculation that Powel Crosley, Jr., worked with other designers on the CRAD. It has been said that Louis Schweitzer, who had worked for Stutz, LeBaron and the Murray Body Company before going to work for Crosley, also worked on the Crosley body. Another possibility was Alex Tremulis, who later designed the Tucker. Tremulis was a likely candidate, as he had experience with small cars, having consulted with Bantam. And certainly the high nose of the final Crosley design echoes that of the late 1930s Hudsons for which Tremulis is often credited. But his contribution seems to have been only six clay models, which Crosley rejected. The bulk of the Crosley's design came

Noted Crosley collector Paul Gorrell owns the original CRAD prototype vehicle, restored and painted its original dove gray. Although it lacks a hood ornament, the CRAD shares elements both from the design patent and from what the Crosley finally turned out to be. The fenders, and the fact that the headlights are mounted on the fenders, are major differences between the CRAD and the production Crosley. Comparing Crosley's crude sketches and the patent drawings with the prototype, and then with the production car, makes an interesting study of the evolution of an automobile from idea to final form. *Photo courtesy of Jim Bollman*

This photo of the CRAD shows even more dramatically the close-set rear wheels. The wrap-around sheet metal of the rear body gives the car a stylish flirt, although the miniature bumper and tiny rear window seem to have been afterthoughts. Crosley referred to it as a "modified teardrop" shape. Although the fenders are understated, the front-end treatment is reminiscent of the Graham Hollywood Sedan, which had full-pontoon fenders. Unlike the production Crosleys, the CRAD had a manual starting mechanism that was similar to those on gasoline lawnmowers. Wrap a rope around the crank, and pull! The hood was shaped to accommodate the pull-starter. *Photo courtesy of Jim Bollman*

This is what the Crosley CRAD looked like in 1992, before it was restored by Paul Gorrell. Gorrell rescued the hulk from a Cincinnati warehouse, along with other interesting items. Restoration took over a year. That's Jim Bollman looking over the car. *Photo courtesy of Jim Bollman*

from the mind of Powel Crosley, Jr., and the drafting pen of Leonard Keller.

Crosley actually built the chassis for the coupe as a one-off, using custom-manufactured components. The result was a rather futuristic-looking vehicle. He spent quite a bit of time "experimenting" with it at his Indiana farm.

Word eventually got out about the CRAD. People saw it on the road, and perhaps one or two of the Crosley Corporation employees involved with it talked. Or it may have been intentionally leaked. Still, neither of the Crosleys would confirm that they were building an automobile, not even when the name "the Crosley Radio Corporation" was changed to "the Crosley Corporation" in 1938, "so that the company will be able, if conditions warrant, to enter the automobile industry when, as and if, such entry into the automobile industry appears desirable," according to a letter to Crosley stockholders.

In October, 1938, *Time* magazine reported that Powel Crosley admitted (their word) to "experimenting on [a] $200 car." Newspapers around the country also wrote that Crosley was developing a car. Crosley lore has

it that the Crosley automobile (the name finally settled on) was supposed to have made its debut in 1938. But a monumental flooding of the Ohio River in January 1937 delayed plans. The car probably wasn't ready for production anyway.

The Crosley's evolution continued into 1939. At some point, the narrow rear track was dropped. Both front and rear treads were now 40 inches. The new design still saved money by eliminating universal joints. Rubber engine mounts were supposed to compensate for the twisting that universal joints protected against.

Despite the continual speculation about a Crosley automobile, nothing official was said about it until March 1939, a month before the formal introduction. In response to a query at a Crosley stockholders' meeting that month, Lewis Crosley allowed that the company "might" have an announcement about the "possibility" of the Crosley Corporation building an automobile in the near future. Then, on April 2, Lewis came clean and announced the specifications of the Crosley automobile.

After decades of detours, Powel Crosley, Jr., was finally going to put an automobile into production. With the resources of the Crosley Corporation behind it, this car would not suffer the fate of its predecessors. Crosley was 100-percent in charge and had all the backing he needed.

For unknown reasons, the Crosley Corporation sent out a press release before the unveiling that described the Crosley as having the 18-inch rear track of the CRAD. Several newspapers picked this up. There still were rumors that the Crosley would be a three-wheeler, too. At a guess, the press releases had been prepared and set aside for the hoped-for 1938 rollout (Crosley never was a patient man). When the time came to send out press releases, someone just grabbed the prepared sheets and away they went.

The final product was the 1939 Crosley automobile as it is known today. It boasted two cylinders, three speeds and four wheels on an 80-inch wheelbase with a 40-inch track. It had 12-inch wheels, with tires 4-1/4 inches wide. The previous curves at the rear end on the CRAD were flared out and small fenders were added to enclose the wheels.

The Crosley's official debut took place on April 20, 1939. It was unveiled at the Indianapolis Motor Speedway to an audience of 200 or so dealers and journalists. The rollout featured at least three Crosleys, plus a bodiless chassis that showed off what the Crosley had inside. Veteran Indy race drivers Louis Meyer, Kelly Petillo and Wilbur Shaw were hired to chauffeur guests around the track in the shiny new Crosleys.

In introducing the Crosley to the assembled group, Powel Crosley, Jr., made a Henry Ford-like statement. "I believe this to be a transportation unit of entirely different conception," he said, "which strikes out for itself to be used with respect and pride by people of moderate means for practical, comfortable transportation and recreation. It also offers utility and secondary transportation to those who can and do afford anything from the lowest-priced car in the general field today, to the highest priced automobile made."

Continued on page 34

This 1939 Crosley coupe (distinguished from the sedan by the curve in the window frame at the upper rear) is parked at the front door of Powel Crosley, Jr.'s, Cincinnati mansion. As can be seen here, the production Crosley did away with the sharp slope in the metal behind the passenger door that was present in the CRAD. This made production less complicated by giving the body a straight belt line to follow. It also made for a simpler base on which to design body styles to come. The semi-circular motorcycle-style front fenders were replaced by deeper pontoon-style fenders. (The front fenders closely resembled those of the 1940 Graham Hollywood Sedan.) The headlight housings were mounted on the engine cowl rather than the fenders, bucking the new trend toward burying lights in fenders. The rear fenders were little more than fender flares, and echoed the rear fenders of the Chrysler Airflow, sans skirts. It was almost as if half-circle fenders were inset into the body, like the newly popular flush-wall radios. *Banks Collection*

The 1939 Crosley is literally unveiled at the Indianapolis Motor Speedway by Powel Crosley, Jr., with the help of two employees and his young grandson, Lew. All but Powel were decked out in coveralls emblazoned with the Crosley logo. Lew smashed a small bottle of gasoline against the nose of one of the cars to christen it. *Banks Collection*

At least three Crosley autos were on hand for the Indianapolis introduction, tops down and ready to roll. *Banks Collection*

More sideline action at Indianapolis Motor Speedway during the Crosley rollout. NBC network announcer Durward Kirby interviews famous flier Roscoe Turner, who would open a Crosley auto dealership as a division of his Roscoe Turner Aeronautical Company in Indianapolis. *Banks Collection*

Radio would of course have been a part of the Crosley automobile's introduction. Here, a pensive-looking Powel Crosley, Jr., is interviewed by the celebrated world traveler and journalist Lowell Thomas over the NBC "Blue" radio network. Crosley would have arranged the mid-day program as a "news event" that was in reality an extended commercial. *Banks Collection*

Waukesha built a 35.39-cubic-inch (580cc) engine with a 3-inch bore and 2-3/4-inch stroke for the Crosley. It put out 13-1/2 horsepower and was a modified version of an engine designed to power an orchard sprayer. The engine was frequently referred to as an "airplane-type," the reference alluding to the fact that it was air-cooled, making use of a "suction blower" that was an integral part of the flywheel to boost airflow. Crosley estimated that the car would "easily" get 50 miles to a gallon of gasoline, at speeds up to 50 miles per hour, although 40 mph was recommended for cruising. Load capacity was 500 pounds (or, if you were talking about using the Crosley as a delivery vehicle, a quarter-ton). *Photo courtesy Jim Bollman*

In addition to the completed cars, the Indianapolis display included a bodiless Crosley chassis. Newspapermen and dealers had the opportunity to examine not only what lay under the hood, but all the details of the car's design, components and assembly. *Photo courtesy Jim Bollman*

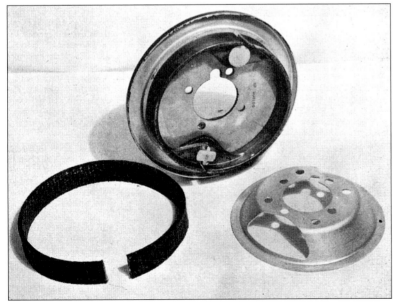

The 1939 Crosley's braking system used a one-piece fabric liner that "floated" between the brake drum and a hub, the hub serving as a 360-degree brake shoe. Both sides of the liner were used in braking, pressed against the drum by the hub. Invented in 1931 by Jesse G. Hawley, the system was known as a "floating lining" brake system. Crosley referred to it as the "neutral-shoe" brake. As with the Waukesha engine, Crosley billed the brakes as "aircraft-type," a sobriquet he used to make anything new even more impressive. The brakes themselves worked very well, having four times as much surface area to operate against as drum brakes. *Photo courtesy Jim Bollman*

Perhaps hinting to the carriage trade, this photo displays a Crosley coupe with Powel Crosley's Fairchild 45-A airplane, at the Crosley estate in Cincinnati. Crosley's daughter, Page, stands next to the aircraft's open door. *Banks Collection*

This straight-on view of a Crosley sedan looks a little alien. It almost seems to be all eyes and nose. *Photo by Bill Angert*

A look at the Crosley's interior in the front. Everything is a bit smaller than it would have been in any other kind of car. The door handles aren't seen here because they were behind the driver's shoulder, but you can see the map pockets in the passenger door. Note the small horn button and optional electric windshield wiper motor. This car has neither heater nor radio The metal plate directly in front of the steering wheel is where the radio would be, had it been ordered from the factory. *Photo courtesy of Bill Angert*

Here's a look at an open door. You can see the sliding glass windows, and the pull-handles for each. The paneling is textured, colored cardboard. Midway down on the right you will see the door handle, located in a difficult spot to reach when the door was closed. The bottom of the door panel opens to map compartments. *Photo by Bill Angert*

The Crosley's dashboard provided an oil pressure gauge, a speedometer with odometer and an ampere gauge, to advise as to the status of the generator and battery. A key lock, a pull-rod to engage the starter, a manual choke and controls for the outside air vents completed the dash. *Photo by Bill Angert*

Looking back from the passenger seat, it is possible to see the driver's door handle, near the top edge of the far door's red lining. Parts of the convertible top support bows are also visible. The seat backs are little more than fabric stretched over bent pipe, while the seat bottoms are a little more substantial. The rear seat consists of a padded bottom and back. Storage space is behind the seat back. The white curve at the right edge of the seat back is the wheel well. *Photo by Bill Angert*

The Crosley's 135-pound, 580-cc, 13-1/2-horsepower engine was an opposed two-cylinder gasoline model, built by Waukesha Motor Company of Waukesha, Wisconsin, a company with plenty of experience building automobile engines. The car had an electric starter. It was air-cooled, like the overwhelming majority of aircraft engines. No water or anti-freeze needed. The transmission was a manual three-speed (with one reverse speed), controlled by an oddly-mounted floor shifter that extended from below the dash at an almost-horizontal angle. This differed from the move by other manufacturers toward mounting gearshifts on steering posts.

Bumper-to-bumper, the Crosley measured 120 inches. It was 47 inches wide, and 56 inches from ground to top—not far off the dimensions of the American Bantam. Road clearance was 7-1/2 inches. The weight was given as 925 pounds, filled with gas and oil. Interior appointments were almost non-existent. No sound-deadening material like felt or jute was included in floors or doors—just paper. Rubber floor mats were standard equipment, as was the inside rearview mirror. The seat cushions were well-padded, while the seat backs consisted of crude fabric or leatherette material stretched across steel pipe framing, with a minimum of padding.

Both the coupe and sedan (the only models available) were convertibles. The tops were made of black fabric with red trim. The windshield was a single piece of flat glass, as opposed to the split windshields popular at the time. Many of the 1939 Crosleys had a hand-operated windshield wiper. The Crosley's dashboard was equipped with a minuscule glove box, plus an ignition lock and a push-pull lever for the manual choke. To engage the starter, one had to pull a rod mounted under the dash. It was sometimes outfitted with a grab-ring. (A very few of the first Crosleys had floor-mounted starter buttons.) If the optional radio was not installed at the factory, the opening for it above the steering column was covered by a steel plate. Ditto the speaker. Instruments were limited to an oil-pressure gauge, a speedometer/odometer and an ammeter. Gas was checked with a dipstick, which was actually a 24-inch ruler that doubled as the hood prop. (A wire hood prop would soon replace the ruler.)

Prices were $325 for the coupe, and $350 for the sedan, exclusive of shipping and federal excise tax. (Shipping averaged $30 to $60, and excise tax was around $10.) Crosley had hoped to keep the price to $300 or less, but it wasn't possible. Available colors were dovegray ("Duv-Gray") or blue. By June a color that some saw as yellow and others said was cream was available at extra cost. The wheels were painted red and sported chromed hubcaps with the Crosley logo in red.

The car was well-received, overall. Some likened the car's appearance to a bathtub, but *Time* magazine called it "a sleek, rakish, convertible sedan with ... a neatly streamlined hood and front end." Included in the streamlining was a small chrome hood ornament with "Crosley" in red on either side. The ornament looked like a piece of Machine Age art, an almost-cylinder about six inches long. In addition to being decorative, it also popped the hood latch when the owner twisted it. On some models, small chrome letters spelled out "Crosley" at the upper the part of the engine cowling on each side, next to the door.

This first line of Crosley automobiles would be called "Series 1A." 1940 models would be called "Series 2A." In 1941 the designation would be "CB41," and 1942 models would be "CB42." The serial number on each car would begin with its series number.

The 1939/40 New York World's Fair opened on April 30, 1939. The Crosley Corporation signed on as an exhibitor in December 1938. Then the company backed out, only to return in April to lease a 3/4-acre site very near the Trylon and Perisphere. At the site, Crosley

The Crosley hood ornament. Twist it and it popped the hood latch.
Photo courtesy Bill Angert

Looking at the Crosley from the rear, you can see the gas filler, spare tire (optional) mount, and the single combination license-plate and stop light. The narrow bumper has crosley painted on it, an indication that when it was manufactured no Crosley emblems were available. *Photo courtesy Bill Angert*

built a two-towered pavilion designed by industrial designer Carl Sundberg, of Sundberg & Ferar in Detroit. (Sundberg would work on Crosley automobiles after World War II.) The Crosley building was in the Communications & Business zone, appropriately located at the corner of Main Street and the Street of Wheels. To celebrate the fair's opening, nine Crosleys bedecked with flags and banners (some of them advertisements) paraded through the city to Flushing Meadows. Each was driven by a young woman.

Some wondered why Crosley wasn't in the Transportation Zone, with Ford and the other automakers. Crosley was better-known as a radio-maker, and there probably was no space left in the Transportation Zone by the time Crosley committed.

In keeping with the fair's "World of Tomorrow" theme, the Crosley Corporation displayed the latest in appliances, its radio/FAX newspaper, the Xervac hair-restorer, television and "The Car of Tomorrow." Several Crosley autos were on display inside and outdoors on the quarter-acre lot behind the pavilion. At certain times, fair visitors could take a spin on a small track designed to demonstrate Crosley autos. They were usually chauffeured by pretty models in World's Fair uniforms.

A small fleet of Crosley automobiles prepares for a caravan across New York to Flushing Meadows and the World's Fair. *Banks Collection*

Everything the Crosley Corporation manufactured was showcased in its World's Fair exhibits. This post card emphasizes the Crosley automobile, and promotes the Shelvador refrigerator-freezer, Crosey's "Press, Jr." model camera (which failed to go to the market), gas and electric ranges, gasoline- and electric-powered washers and dryers, ironers and radios. *Banks Collection*

A portion of the Crosley Pavilion at the 1939/40 New York World's Fair. The quarter acre enclosed by the picket fence included a winding asphalt-paved trail on which "Crosley Glamor-Tone Gals" drove Crosleys filled with fairgoers. *Banks Collection*

A uniformed attendant sees off a happy guest in a Crosley sedan at the 1940 New York World's Fair. *Banks Collection*

A 1940 Crosley coupe (distinguished from the sedan by the curved window frame at the top rear) awaits passengers at the New York World's Fair. It sports the optional windshield wiper and storage boot for the top. *Banks Collection*

Here, Powel Crosley, Jr., takes a spin with the ladies to show that his 6-foot, 4-inch frame can fit into the Crosley—along with his hat. *Banks Collection*

Rather than have to develop a nationwide network of dealers, Crosley hoped that a significant number of existing Crosley radio and appliance dealers would take on the car. It would give the Crosley yet another "different" aspect. There were some 25,000 Crosley dealers in all, but most of them were small- or medium-sized operations like hardware and furniture stores. Many did not have room for an automobile, and providing service was often out of the question. The same was true of taking trade-ins.

Still, some large Crosley retailers did jump on the bandwagon. The Crosley went on sale at Macy's New York department store on June 19, 1939. One car was displayed in the store's Broadway window. A second car, along with a bare chassis, could be seen in the basement. That first day netted 14 orders. Mrs. Averell Harriman bought two. Major department stores in other cities, like Bamberger's in Newark, New Jersey, Christman's in Joplin and the May Company in Cleveland, also sold Crosley automobiles. Such establishments typically made arrangements with garages in their locales to handle preparation and service. By the time the Crosley reached the department stores, prices had gone up to $350 for the coupe and $375 for the sedan.

Crosley distributors took up some of the slack, "fishing" for dealers to sell the car with newspaper advertisements in addition to direct sales calls. Crosley's own distribution company set up offices and a showroom at 155 East 44th Street in New York City in mid-July. The distributorship rented the entire first and second floors of the building. But there still weren't enough dealers willing or able to sell automobiles, in Powel Crosley, Jr.'s opinion. So when the 1941 models were announced (in July 1940), Crosley invited a broader range of retailers to take on the car. This second round of Crosley automobile dealers came from the ranks of those who sold other makes, such as Packard, Hudson, and Willys. Used-car dealerships and filling stations also found the little car an easy fit. A few dealerships opened to sell the Crosley exclusively.

The first cars on display were probably hand-assembled at Crosley's Cincinnati factory. Press reports about the introduction often implied that the car was not yet in production. Nor were engines available in quantity in April. On May 2, 1939, the *Milwaukee Sentinel* reported that Waukesha had just begun work on two orders of 5,000 motors each for Crosley. The first 5,000 were expected to be completed by the end of July.

A half-page newspaper ad alerts Macy's shoppers to the 1939 advent of the Crosley in New York. Major emphasis is placed on "name" parts suppliers. Association with industry giants like Autolite, Goodrich, Timken and Delco couldn't hurt, and implied that the Crosley automobile was of equal quality and legitimacy. *Banks Collection*

Two department store shoppers look over a Crosley displayed on what looks to be either artificial turf or real sod. It appears that there was at least one Crosley of each color (blue and gray) in stock. *Photo courtesy of the May Company*

Male customers at the May Company in Cleveland crowd around to pop the hood and check out the Crosley's engine. Immediately noticeable is the gas tank, which held 4-1/4 gallons. Gasoline was gravity-fed except in deluxe models, which had fuel pumps and a tank in the rear. Fuel level was checked with a wooden dipstick. Note the six-volt battery. The tiny engine itself is hidden in this shot; all you can see is the air filter. *Photo courtesy of the May Company*

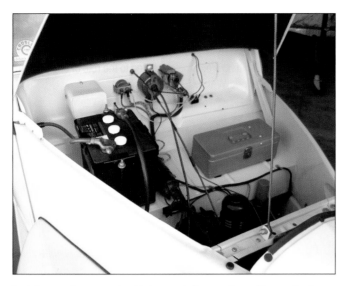

In deluxe sedans room had to be made for a radio, so the gas tank was mounted under the rear of the car, and an electric fuel pump added. With this setup there was space to keep a tool box. At the extreme right is the shelf on which the radio would have been mounted, and the cover plate over the opening through which the radio would extend into the cabin. *Photo by Bill Angert*

The Richmond plant was in full production in August, however. As quickly as cars came off the line they were shipped to dealers in Indiana, Ohio, Illinois, Nebraska, Texas, Iowa, Pennsylvania, New York, Wisconsin and Massachusetts, among other states. The Crosleys that traveled the farthest to U.S. soil were those shipped to Bazaar Auto Sales, in Sitka, Alaska Territory. Many went by rail; the Crosleys were short enough that they could be loaded into a standard boxcar sideways. Total 1939 production was 2,017 cars. (20 years later, about 500 of these would still be in operation, according to the *Service Motors Bulletin*. Today, about 100 pre-War vehicles are extant.)

Advertising was on-and-off. There were no concerted campaigns like those of major manufacturers Ford, General Motors and Chrysler. Some radio spots appeared on WLW and programs it fed NBC. National magazine advertising was minimal at first. A lot of attention was given to "co-op" newspaper advertising, in which dealers placed prepared co-op ads (paid-for in part by Crosley) to newspapers. This was the same approach used to advertise Crosley radios. To a certain extent the car's novelty insured free advertising; newspapers and magazines hardly could ignore this wonder, whether Crosley bought ads or not. Apparently just enough was spent on advertising to help keep the free publicity rolling.

Continued on page 46

A closer look at the engine itself reveals that there is plenty of room under the hood. This view is taken leaning over the fender on the driver's side, looking forward. The parallel lines at the left are part of the grille opening, and you can see pavement in front of the engine. *Photo by Bill Angert*

Perhaps the most interesting model for 1940 was the station wagon. Sliding-glass windows graced not only the doors, but the rear body on each side, as well. Opera windows were set into the upper of the two rear doors, which were clamshell-type. The upper half of the back opened upward, while the lower half opened downward, like a pickup's tailgate. Reduced to simply the front end and cargo box, it was the same vehicle as the Covered Wagon. Or, to look at it another way, the Covered Wagon was a soft-top version of the station wagon. *Banks Collection*

This 1940 Crosley coupe displays several options, including the radio and antenna, the driver-side electric windshield wiper, rear seat and top boot. Note the rubber floor mats (standard) and the open air vent below the antenna. Cardboard covered the sides of the cabin to cut down on road noise, and each door was adorned with a map pocket. *Banks Collection*

Powel Crosley's daughter, Page, and her son, Lew, pose with a new Crosley wood-bodied station wagon in 1940. You can see the fabric covering the wood roof. To the right it is possible to make out the sliding windows installed in the side. The black object just in front of the steering wheel is the windshield wiper motor. The simple structure of the driver's seat is easy to see. *Photo courtesy of Norm Luppino*

Looking back from the front passenger seat of a Crosley station wagon, the warm glow of the maple interior is evident. Note the sliding glass windows on the side. *Photo courtesy Jim Bollman*

AUTOMOBILES

"PARKWAY" DELIVERY

Smart, all metal, package delivery car for the up-to-date merchant. Cuts small delivery costs in half. Low first cost, and real savings daily on gas and oil. Designed for speedy, efficient deliveries with minimum effort. Power incredible in so small a car. Proven economy of gasoline mileage. Check over its specifications.

$350
AT RICHMOND, IND.
FEDERAL TAX EXTRA

ACCESSORIES DESIGNED FOR CROSLEY CARS

SPECIAL PUSH BUTTON AUTO RADIO
Remarkable performance and fine tone. Compact 5-tube superheterodyne, concealed two unit receiver with improved push button tuning, illuminated call letters, slide rule type dial, automatic volume control.

REAR SEAT—Comfortable full width leather fabric seat, including back support, is attractively upholstered. Added to coupe makes a four passenger sedan. Easy to remove. Station Wagon rear seat has special wood support.

TOP BOOT—Top may be neatly and securely enclosed with attractively finished black covering.

TONNEAU COVER—Snap-on 3-ply sport topping smartly covers entire rear deck.

BAGGAGE RACK—Converts rear of coupe or sedan for light delivery work. Strong slatted oak floor boards will withstand hard usage.

GOODRICH TIRE
Metal disc wheel with 4-ply Goodrich 4.25x12 tire, lock and two keys.

BOULEVARD LIGHTS
Adds a touch of distinctiveness that cannot be overemphasized. Well made, black enameled, nickel mounted with two beveled glasses.

The Crosley Parkway Delivery had a removable fabric top over the driver and passenger cabin, but from the doors back it was all wood. The idea was to protect cargo with a secure compartment accessible only from the front seat. There were no doors or windows in the rear. This Parkway Delivery featured an external mirror. *Banks Collection*

Added to the options list for 1940 were a push-button radio, a boot for the convertible top, a removable rear seat and a slatted wood baggage rack to fit in place of the rear seat. The "boulevard light" option was strictly for the panel delivery; one would be mounted on the curbside, to light the driver's way to a home or business where he was making a delivery. Note the radio position: This meant that the "concealed" radio receiver chassis rested in the space normally taken up by the gas tank, which in turn meant that the gas tank was located lower and required a fuel pump. The relocated tank was beneath the body at the rear. It held six gallons. The spare tire, which was mounted on the car's rear bumper, came with a locking mechanism and two keys. The line was expanded with a wood-bodied station wagon and a panel delivery model. Wood body elements were contracted out to the Rider Furniture Company of Monticello, Indiana. Rider was owned by an acquaintance of Crosley's who also owned the company that made boxes for Crosley Radio. *Banks Collection*

A closer look at the 1940 coupe reveals the details of the sliding door windows. "Aircraft glass" 1/8th of an inch thick was used, and correspondingly narrow tracks made replacement difficult. Outside air was also brought in by an external vent just ahead of the front door. *Photo courtesy of the May Company*

Ray Milland chats with Paulette Goddard, who is sitting in her Crosley sedan. A Crosley like this one was used in the duo's 1943 movie, *The Crystal Ball*. The car in the movie has its B pillars and cant rails removed, and with them the door windows. The spare wheel is mounted on the rear, but it is missing the tire. Other Hollywood celebrities who owned pre-War Crosleys included Humphrey Bogart, Fred Waring and Gloria Swanson. *Banks Collection*

In addition to new models and options, 1940 saw new engineering talent added to the Crosley Corporation. Lewis M. Clement was brought in from RCA to oversee the Crosley Corporation's engineering and research in general. At the same time, Chrysler's superintendent of planning, John D. Moran, moved to Crosley. Crosley also hired several sales executives from competing companies.

Most importantly, a new engineer headed the Crosley Corporation's automobile division. He was Paul Klotsch, a German aeronautical and automotive engineer who had been a flier in von Richtofen's "Flying Circus" during World War I. Powel Crosley hired him away from the Briggs Manufacturing Company (a major maker of auto bodies for Ford), where he was an experimental engineer. (Klotsch had also worked for the Chance Vought Corporation.) One of the first things Klotsch did to improve the Crosley was to add a universal joint. The car had been breaking driveshafts (and, it is rumored, some bellhousings). Further, he altered some suspension elements and switched the brake system to a conventional Bendix drum-and-riveted-shoe configuration. The original braking system, manufactured by the Hawley Brake Corporation, used a 360-degree band of heat-resistant material rather than elliptical shoes; however, it had proved to be problematic. Perhaps the brake band had a tendency to get stuck against the drum, or entangle itself. No one is certain. (The band was composed of yarn impregnated with graphite.)

Klotsch also de-stroked the engine. This lowered the car's horsepower to 12, but made the engine more reliable and stopped it breaking crankshafts. Three-position seats were introduced. The 1940 was an improved car overall, and cheaper to build. But only 422 1940 models went out the door. The decreased production was in part due to phasing in the new elements. In addition, the model "year" was shortened by a marketing ploy, which found Crosley announcing its 1941 models in July 1940 instead of waiting until fall as was traditional among auto manufacturers.

Something else new in 1940 was the Crosmobile. This was the trademarked export name for the Crosley automotive line, to prevent confusion with a prominent English carmaker named Crossley, who exported autos and buses to countries of the British Empire and elsewhere. The differences in the export versions were the replacement of the Crosley name with Crosmobile on the front emblem, hubcaps, instruments and radio. Depending on where Crosmobiles were shipped, some were right-hand drive. Crosmobiles showed up in many of the countries where Crosley radios, refrigerators and other appliances were sold—as nearby as Canada and as far away as Japan.

Some pre-War Crosmobiles made it as far as China. After World War II ended, at least two foreign-service officers in China filed claims for the loss of their Crosmobiles, which were appropriated by Japan's occupying army. (Each was granted partial compensation by the State Department.) Crosmobiles were also seen in England.

Scene from *Abbott and Costello in Hollywood* (1945). Lou Costello is a deliveryman with a Crosley Parkway Delivery. The odd look of the little Parkway Delivery fit comedic situations well. *Photo courtesy Crosley Automobile Club*

A happy pre-War Crosley owner with his dog. A close look will reveal the chrome "Crosley" letters at the upper rear of the engine cowl, next to the door line. The hood ornament is also lettered "Crosley" in red on both sides. *Photo courtesy Keith Beecher*

The standard Crosley pre-War coupe. In this illustration you can make out what looks like a hint of a running board, beginning at the base of the front fender. The mini-running board was there to brace the fender; without it, vibration from the engine was cracking front fenders. *Banks Collection*

An example of the pre-War Crosley logo. A stylized bolt of electricity or radio waves run through the word "Crosley." *Banks Collection*

CHAPTER 4

1941-1944: Wartime

The 1941 Crosley range included just about every sort of body that could be dreamed up for the Crosley chassis. There were seven models in all, and the price was rolled back on the coupe. Here are the prices for each at the beginning of the model year (mid-1940), followed by the prices in May 1941:

- Coupe – Convertible, $299, $325
- Standard Sedan – Convertible, $349, $375 (DeLuxe Convertible Sedan – $385)
- Parkway Delivery – Steel cargo compartment, fabric cabin top, $375, $399
- Pick-up Delivery – Wood sides and top, $385, $399
- Covered Wagon – Fabric top and cargo compartment covering, $399, $425
- Panel Delivery – Wood sides and top, $435, $449
- Station Wagon – Wood sides and top, $450, $479

For comparison, here's a sampling of prices for comparable 1941 vehicles from other manufacturers, all of them larger than Crosleys, of course:

- Ford Coupe – $730
- Plymouth Sedan – $769 (Special Plymouth Sedan - $845)
- Ford Business Coupe – $769
- Chevrolet Pickup Truck – $600
- Hudson Pickup Truck – $600
- Plymouth Panel Delivery – $720
- Packard One-Ten Deluxe Station Wagon (wood body) – $1,236

Crosley prices would continue to rise as the model year progressed, with the Panel Delivery reaching as high as $449, and the Station Wagon $479.

As this May 1941 advertisement indicates, Crosley expanded its range of personal and commercial vehicles to present itself as being every bit as varied a carmaker as any. In reality, each of the models used the same chassis, engine and front end. The only differences were between the rear of the doors and the back bumper. The creativity behind these new designs was likely as much that of Paul Klotsch and other engineers as it was Crosley's. Powel Crosley almost never gave credit to anyone else. *Banks Collection*

Crosley's Parkway Delivery was an eye-catching vehicle. The only access to the cargo compartment was from the inside (like trunk access in early Nash Metropolitans). With its configuration, it was not likely loaded beyond its capacity of 500 pounds. Crosley liked to recommend it as a delivery vehicle for florists, pharmacies and bakeries. It may even have been used to sneak a non-paying guest into a drive-in movie now and then. *Banks Collection*

More was new in the 1941 Crosleys than the body designs. Notable among the improvements were a "constant mesh" starter, an improved oiling system, self-equalizing brakes, a large crankshaft and larger main bearings. Engineers relocated the parking brake handle, apparently the source of complaints from Crosley owners. The parking brake utilized elements of a Paul Klotsch patent that involved a vertical pull rod rather than the usual hand lever (U.S. Patent No. 2,309,734). Advertising claimed better fuel economy and faster hill-climbing for the new models, too. An improved ignition system invented by Klotsch also may have been incorporated in the '41 model. (See U.S. Patent No. 2,330,431.)

The 1941 coupe and sedan looked pretty much like their 1940 predecessors. The 1941 DeLuxe Convertible Sedan, which cost ten dollars more than the Standard Sedan, was dressed up a bit with stainless-steel trim

under the windshield and on the A-pillars, and may have included an option or two.

In an odd development, the Crosley Corporation announced in January 1941 that it would be "adding a powered tricycle to its automotive line." Shades of 1938's rumors! But rather than having a single wheel in the rear and two in front, this vehicle was a three-wheeled motorcycle. It had a sturdy pipe frame, solid disc wheels and was powered by the now-famous Waukesha two-cylinder engine. The engine was surrounded by a sheet-metal cover, preventing contact between the rider and hot metal. A shaft drive propelled the rear wheels.

At the same time, the Crosley Corporation announced that it was working on a 15-foot boat powered by an inboard engine. Details were that the engine would be a version of the Waukesha that powered Crosley automobiles, with a water-cooled head. It would produce

This 1941 Crosley pickup truck (built in 1940) was put into service as a "track safety car" at the Indianapolis Motor Speedway. It was equipped with the latest in fire-extinguishing equipment. Note the canvas top, held on with snaps. This was another Crosley money-saving tactic, fabric being cheaper than steel. The pickup truck was a natural evolution of the Covered Wagon and Station Wagon. In these two photos the pickup is parked in front of the pagoda-like Timing Stand. *Banks Collection*

Another view of the 1941 Crosley pickup truck. From the doors forward, it is a twin of the Crosley sedan. Note the wood bed—three planks high—and the wood fender surrounds at the rear, carried over from the 1940 Crosley station wagon. Later pickups would have all-metal beds. This may be a prototype. Or, the Indy track owners may have bought a plain chassis and had the cargo box (bed) built. Production models had a steel cargo box and drop-down metal tailgate. *Banks Collection*

Makes Automobile History

ON HIS 6,517 MILE TRANSCONTINENTAL RUN

in a New Standard 1941 Stock Model

CROSLEY

COVERED WAGON

In September 1941, Ervin "Cannonball" Baker took a trip across the United States in a new Crosley Covered Wagon to publicize the Crosley's reliability and superior gasoline mileage. Baker and a partner drove the Crosley 6,517.3 miles and used 129.25 gallons of gas. The average came to 50.4 miles per gallon, and the total cost for gas was $29.37. The route took Baker from Cincinnati to Los Angeles, and then back across the country to New York. Newspapers along Baker's route did stories and Crosley published a brochure publicizing the trip and the car's performance. *Banks Collection*

Panel Delivery $435.00*

The Crosley Panel Delivery was like the Station Wagon—but without the side windows, and no back seat. The rear doors were vertical, each with a small window. Early versions had a wood top and sides. Later versions had a wood top with fabric covering it. *Photo courtesy of Jim Bollman*

Station Wagon $450.00*

The Crosley Station Wagon was another attention-getter. It was a lot like the Crosley Pick-Up Delivery with wood sides and a fabric-covered wood roof added. It used the same cargo box and tailgate as the pickup truck, and the upper portion of the tailgate opened upward, like a clamshell. *Photo courtesy of Jim Bollman*

This 1941 Crosley station wagon has been completely restored. The red wheels were a factory feature. The fabric top covers wooden bows and liner. Replace the side and rear windows with steel and you have a panel delivery. This wagon has an optional rearview mirror outside the driver's window. It also has the CROSLEY lettering on the front fender panel just ahead of the doors and below the hood.

The Crosley three-wheeled motorcycle had telescoping front forks, a back seat with grab-bars for riders, plus a forward-facing footrest on each side. Rear wheels were 12 inches in diameter, while the front wheel was 15. The gearshift was mounted next to the driver's seat, and the rear brakes were operated by a foot pedal on the right side. The front brake, accelerator and clutch were operated with handlebar controls. Announced at the beginning of 1941, the trike was developed in 1940. At least two are in the hands of private collectors today. *Michael Banks collection*

10 horsepower at 2,800 rpm. Word was that the boat would be manufactured at a new plant in Miami, Florida. This was a project largely handled by Crosley's son, Powel Crosley, III. For some years he had made boats his primary interest. The Crosley boat's hull was to be made of three-ply plastic.

Civilian vehicle production continued throughout 1941. In an attempt to boost sales that echoed Powel Crosley's auto accessories marketing, individuals were also offered the opportunity to become Crosley "driver/agents." This meant that someone who bought a car had the right to sell new Crosleys, and get a small discount on their initial purchase.

The 1942 models were announced in the fall. Two of the models were new, and with them Crosley found a way to turn the gathering clouds of war into a mar-

View of the Crosley tricycle from the rear. The same padded seating and grab bars would eventually turn up on the Crosley "Army Car" and the CT-3 "Pup," described later in this chapter. At least two of these were built. *Photo courtesy of the Crosley Automobile Club*

The Crosley "Liberty Sedan" was built in limited numbers, largely as an attention-getter. It was certainly a good-looking car, next to Crosley's canvas-covered coupes and sedans. It is possible that it might have cost Crosley some sales, because it looked so good that those who couldn't afford its $545 price tag were dissuaded from buying the cheaper model when they compared the two. Because of wartime shortages of chromium and other materials, the bumpers and hubcaps were painted. *Michael Banks collection*

keting tool. The first new model was the "Victory Coupe," which appears to have been the same car as the 1940 coupe, but with a catchier name and perhaps some options. The second was the steel-topped "Liberty Sedan." The Liberty Sedan would be the only prewar Crosley vehicle with an all-steel roof, a fact that Crosley made much of. The car featured an "opera window" on each side. Supposedly only 30 were built. The price was $545. It may well have been a marketing device.

Print advertisements for each of the new models shouted slogans like "For Maximum Defense Economy" and "Here's the ONE answer the Government Demands for Maximum Curtailment of Gasoline." It was a subtle attempt to make driving a Crosley seem

more patriotic, which, if you were interested in saving gasoline for the war effort, it was. In advertising for the Liberty Sedan, Crosley managed to suggest that, even though the Liberty Sedan used more steel than other Crosley autos, it was conserving valuable resources. Ads for the Liberty Sedan and Victory Coupe also made heavy use of graphics shaped like official-looking government shields. Those images and the slogans combined to imply a vague sort of official government approval or association. It was no worse than Crosley telling auto owners twenty years before that attaching his "Little Fiend" gadget to their carburetors would let them use water in place of gasoline.

In 1941, the U.S. Navy had approached the Crosley

A beautifully restored Crosley Liberty sedan. Note the outside mirror. The top was not made to be removed. *Photo courtesy of Jim Bollman*

Corporation about what its role would be in war production. Plans were being made for who would build tanks, airplanes, engines, guns and the thousands of other items, great and small, that would be required to win the war that everyone knew was coming. Even before the War Production Board (WPB) began expanding and converting the nation's industrial assets, it was decided that Crosley would work in areas both within and outside of its specialties. It was almost a foregone conclusion that the Crosley Corporation would build radio transmitting and receiving equipment for military use. It also would go to work producing a top-secret device called the radio proximity fuze.

The proximity fuze was a clever, sophisticated and very complex device that multiplied the accuracy of gunners tremendously. Rather than require a shell shot at, say, an enemy aircraft to actually hit that aircraft, the proximity fuze sensed the distance between it and the target, and detonated the shell when it was close enough to damage or destroy the target. In the estimation of top-level military commanders, the proximity fuze was second only to the atomic bomb in its importance in ending World War II.

The Crosley Corporation was building these fuzes—in fact, it built over 20 million of them—at its Cincinnati plant, completely separate from the radio production and other activities going on there. (WLW and WSAI's studios were moved out very soon after the Top Secret project was initiated.) Much of the Crosley plant in Richmond was given over to the production

of gunner canopies for Martin PBY4 bomber/patrol aircraft.

Proximity fuze production was so secret that Powel Crosley, Jr., himself, was not permitted in the section of the Crosley complex where the devices were constructed. Nor was he aware of what the project was. Lewis Crosley interfaced with the contract administrators and engineers, and managed fuze production. Powel did manage to continue operating the automobile line at the Richmond plant—until February 1942, when all civilian motor vehicle production ceased.

Like nearly everyone in America, Powel Crosley knew that war was coming long before it happened. He was thinking about the effects of the war in Europe at least as early as 1940 and how, even without the United States entering the war, materials would become more difficult to obtain, and that consumers would spend less. Therefore, even as plans were being made for the 1942 Crosley automobiles, Crosley put Paul Klotsch and other engineers to work designing military vehicles based on the Crosley 80-inch chassis and Waukesha engine combination. He began sketching ideas for alternate versions of the existing Crosley automobile and other vehicles that suggested themselves, based on his background in aviation and other fields. It was from this thinking that the three-wheel motorcycle grew—along with ideas for a two-wheel cycle.

Like anything Crosley, the motorcycle stood out. Its fuel tank was part of the rear fender. Or, depending on how you viewed it, it *was* the rear fender. It used the two-cylinder Waukesha engine, where most small motorcycles had single-cylinder engines. (The big brutes like the Indian and Harley-Davidson of course had two cylinders, or more.) Even the frame was different. One model had a fork only on the left side in the front, and on the right side at the rear. This gave the Crosley motorcycle a different look, but the real purpose was to make changing wheels easier. It didn't hurt that the configuration used less material. The controls of the two-wheeled bike were like those of the three-wheeler, foot brake, high hand-shifter and all. Also like the three-wheeler, it used a shaft drive.

Crosley turned the first motorcycle prototypes over to the Army for evaluation in the fall of 1940. The Army ran the three-wheeler some 2,000 miles in rough country in Georgia, and it performed admirably. Based on its testing of the bikes, the Army requested certain modifications. Crosley engineers went to work on the changes and resubmitted the motorcycles in January

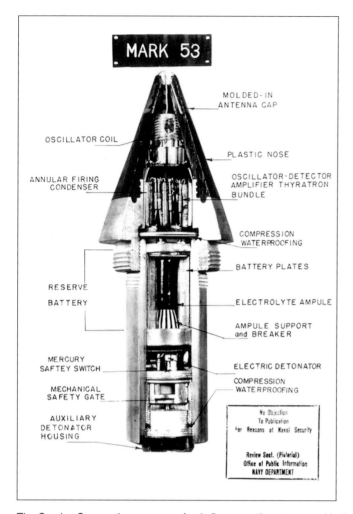

MARK 53

MOLDED-IN
ANTENNA CAP

OSCILLATOR COIL

PLASTIC NOSE

OSCILLATOR-DETECTOR
AMPLIFIER THYRATRON
BUNDLE

ANNULAR FIRING
CONDENSER

COMPRESSION
WATERPROOFING

BATTERY PLATES

RESERVE
BATTERY

ELECTROLYTE AMPULE

AMPULE SUPPORT
and BREAKER

MERCURY
SAFTEY SWITCH

ELECTRIC DETONATOR

MECHANICAL
SAFETY GATE

COMPRESSION
WATERPROOFING

AUXILIARY
DETONATOR
HOUSING

No Objection
To Publication
For Reasons of Naval Security

Review Sect. (Pictorial)
Office of Public Information
NAVY DEPARTMENT

The Crosley Corporation was one of only five operations to assemble the top-secret radio proximity fuze. This was a miniature radio transmitter/receiver that caused anti-aircraft shells to detonate when it sensed a target in close proximity. They were first used in the war in the Pacific, more than tripling ships' gunners' effectiveness against Japanese aircraft. *Photo by Michael Banks*

1941. Concurrent with this, the aforementioned press announcement about the three-wheeler going into production was made. There followed several rounds of testing and requests for changes. At least five motorcycles were made, but none went into production.

At about the same time that Crosley was designing motorcycles, the American Bantam Company was preparing to collaborate with the U.S. Army on a design for a small four-wheel drive vehicle, the Bantam Reconnaissance Car, or BRC. It eventually became the Jeep. Crosley may have known of this, and it could have inspired his next project: a variation on the Crosley coupe that he called an "Army car" or "scout car." (It was occasionally referred to as a "reconnaissance car," maybe out of hope.) Or he may have developed the Army car on his own initiative. As with the motorcycles, it could be a key to getting government development money and

keeping Crosley automotive activities going.

The idea of the Army car was a vehicle that could be used to move small numbers of troops quickly in the field, and serve reconnaissance duties. His concept vehicle looked like a basic Crosley sedan without a top, doors, or sides, powered by the same two-cylinder Waukesha engine used in production Crosleys. Driver and passenger seating was the same as in all Crosleys. The back seat was a bench on which passengers could ride facing the front or rear, with grab bars on either side. In reality, the Mosquito was a hybrid of two existing Crosley vehicles. From the windshield forward it was the same as a Crosley coupe. From behind the driver to the rear it was the same as the three-wheel motorcycle. Yet another example of Crosley money-saving tactics.

The Army requested a prototype, which was delivered to Fort Holabird, Maryland, in May 1940, where it was

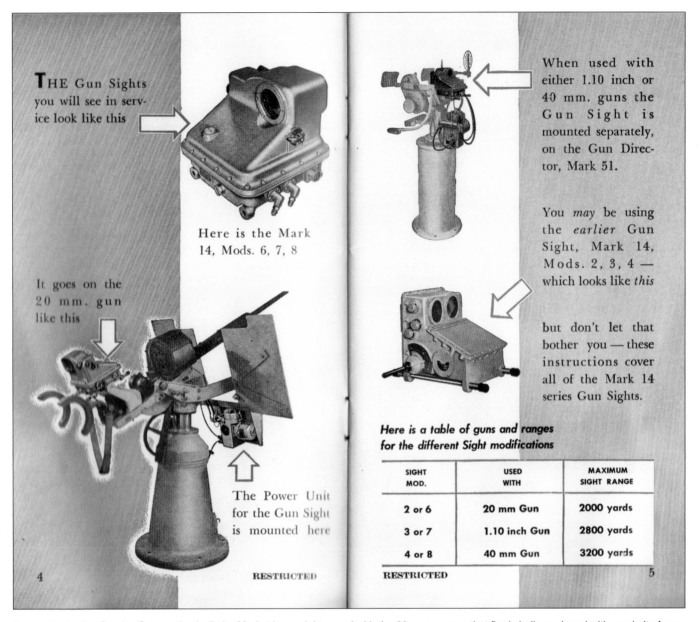

THE Gun Sights you will see in service look like this

Here is the Mark 14, Mods. 6, 7, 8

It goes on the 20 mm. gun like this

The Power Unit for the Gun Sight is mounted here

When used with either 1.10 inch or 40 mm. guns the Gun Sight is mounted separately, on the Gun Director, Mark 51.

You *may* be using the *earlier* Gun Sight, Mark 14, Mods. 2, 3, 4 — which looks like *this*

but don't let that bother you — these instructions cover all of the Mark 14 series Gun Sights.

Here is a table of guns and ranges for the different Sight modifications

SIGHT MOD.	USED WITH	MAXIMUM SIGHT RANGE
2 or 6	20 mm Gun	2000 yards
3 or 7	1.10 inch Gun	2800 yards
4 or 8	40 mm Gun	3200 yards

RESTRICTED

RESTRICTED

4

5

Appropriately, the Crosley Corporation built the Mark 14 gun sights used with the 20-mm cannon that fired shells equipped with proximity fuzes. *Michael Banks collection*

informally dubbed the Mosquito. Crosley also offered his Covered Wagon for the Army to test.

Despite having wholeheartedly embraced the Jeep, the Army did not immediately write off the Crosley Mosquito and Covered Wagon. At the Army's request, Crosley Motors produced an unknown number of each for shipment to Camp McCoy (now Fort McCoy) in Monroe County, Wisconsin. At times a training center for mobile units—beginning with horse-drawn artillery in the 1800s—the post supported mechanized units and was deemed an appropriate testing ground for motorized vehicles like the Mosquito and Covered Wagon.

In February 1942, the Crosley Corporation ceased

producing civilian motor vehicles. Since beginning production early in 1939, the company had turned out 5,757 Crosley cars and trucks. Although much of the plant was changed over to building gun turrets for Martin PBY aircraft, vehicle production did not cease entirely; Powel Crosley, Jr., was a long way from running out of ideas for military vehicles and he was not about to let the automotive operation stand idle, especially not with more government development money to be had. In addition to producing and selling equipment to the military, there were bonanzas in government-sponsored product development, as well as in machinery and facilities acquisitions.

The Crosley two-wheel motorcycle. Powered by a Waukesha 12-horsepower engine, it was more than fast enough. True to Crosley's habit of giving his products unusual features, the gas tank was in the rear fender. The extra weight on the rear wheel would have increased traction, but it didn't affect the rider's control. The engine was surrounded by a sheet-metal cover, which prevented rider contact with hot metal. Front and rear had single forks to make it easier to change wheels. This saved material, as well as precluding placing the gas tank there. Note the foot brake and the hand gearshift on the right side of the seat; the controls were the same as those of the three-wheeler. *Michael Banks collection*

While the Mosquito and Covered Wagon were still being tested at Camp McCoy, Crosley engineers began design work on a lightweight four-wheel drive vehicle. It was officially designated the "CT-3 Scout Car." ("CT" may have stood for "Crosley Transport.")

Informally, the scout car was called the Crosley "Bull Pup," and later simply the "Pup." The nickname might have been inspired by the Crosley Pup of the 1920s, a popular one-tube radio receiver. Then again,

the name may have come from the U.S. Marine Corps, who first tested the car at Quantico, Virginia, in April 1942. A Bulldog is the Corps' mascot, and the CT-3's small size would have suggested "Pup." An often-used Crosley publicity photo of the era shows a squad of Marines lifting the vehicle into the side cargo hatch of a Marine DC-3.

The Pup looked like a miniature Jeep. It was based on the Crosley auto chassis and powered by a 12-horse-

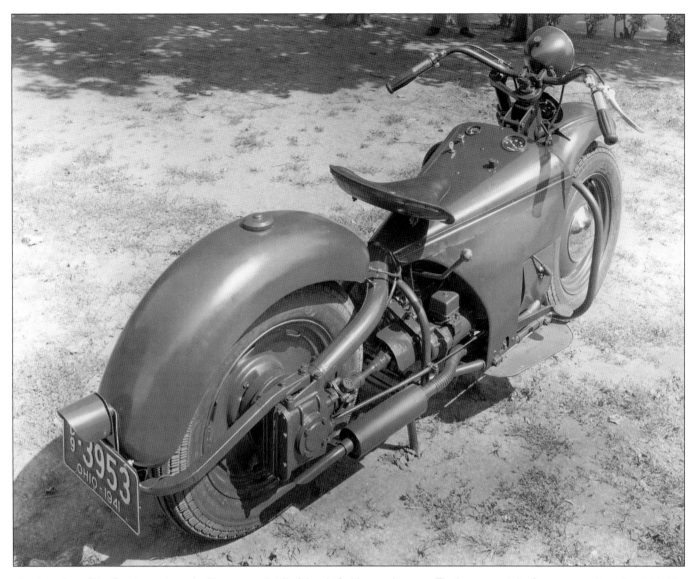

Another view of the Crosley motorcycle. Here, more detail of the shaft drive can be seen. The heavy rear tube frame runs only on the right side. The motorcycle had an electric starter but could be started using a rope on a lawnmower-style pulley at the front of the engine. This had to be included because there was no kick-start. The earliest model had a crude gas tank/rear fender with squared-off sides. Another version had a big hump at the apex of the fender, giving it an ungainly appearance. In the version shown here, the tank has a uniform shape. The Crosley motorcycle was strictly a one-person ride, and it could be tricky. A flywheel on the drive shaft tended to act like a gyroscope, and tried to keep the motorcycle moving in one direction or another. *Michael Banks collection*

power Crosley Waukesha engine "of improved design." The four-wheel-drive Pup had a special transfer case that gave it six forward and two reverse speeds, and featured dual universal joints. Minimal interior fittings saved weight and money. So did fenders made from stiffened canvas. (They were somewhat reminiscent of the leather mudguards on early 1900s automobiles.)

The Pup was intended to provide rapid transportation on the battlefield, and to be easily transportable itself. The small size was dictated by the Crosley chassis, but it also fit a desire on the Army's part for a vehicle light

enough to drop by parachute, something not practical with a Jeep. Fully fueled, the Pup weighed about 1,000 pounds—less than half the weight of the Jeep. At the same time, its cargo capacity was less than 1/3 that of the Jeep's.

Due to the Pup's narrow track and short wheelbase, it could carry only two or three passengers. At that, things were cramped; in one model the passenger sat beside and slightly behind the driver, with his legs extended next to the driver's seat. A second passenger might fit

conituned on page 65

An earlier model of the Crosley military motorcycle. This one has twin front forks, and a fatter gas tank. *Banks Collection*

The 60-mph speedometer on each Crosley motorcycle was a leftover from Crosley automobile stock. It had a speedometer from a prewar Crosley, which only went up to 60 miles per hour. Paul Gorrell relates, however, that on a high-speed run he was able to take the speedometer up to 60, then accelerate all the way around the dial to 60 again. *Photo by Bill Angert*

The Crosley "Army car" was a standard Crosley chassis and front end, built without doors, rear body or top—just a big seating area with grab-bar—a design element that it shared with the Crosley trike and some Crosley Pups. In this configuration, the car could carry four fully-equipped soldiers who, not having to deal with doors or other obstructions, could get in and out (or on and off) of the car quickly. (From behind the driver back, it was the same as the Crosley motorcycle.) In September the Mosquito would be compared with Bantam's BRC, but only briefly. Larger than the Crosley, with more horsepower and a higher ground clearance, the BRC would be chosen over the Mosquito as the Army's general-purpose vehicle for exactly those reasons. The BRC would eventually be termed a General Purpose vehicle, which was quickly shortened to "GP," pronounced "Jeep." Courtesy of the Crosley Automobile Club

Powel Crosley offered the Crosley Covered Wagon alongside his Crosley Army reconnaissance car. The covered wagon was tested by the U.S. Army in Wisconsin. While it resembled larger troop transports, it was too small to be effective in that role and its quarter-ton payload capacity didn't make it feasible as a supply truck. *Courtesy of the Crosley Automobile Club*

This photo shows a squad of U.S. Marines at Cincinnati's Lunken Airport, loading a Crosley CT-3 onto a DC-3 through a side cargo door. From there it was flown to Quantico, Virginia, for testing. *Michael Banks collection*

The Crosley CT-3 "Pup" on display at the Mighty 8th Air Force Heritage Museum outside Savannah, Georgia. The Pup had four 4-inch by 16-inch wheels to help it get around in rugged terrain. (At least one six-wheel version was built, according to Paul Gorrell.) *Photo by Michael Banks*

The Crosley Pup's interior was Spartan, to say the least. *Photo by Michael Banks*

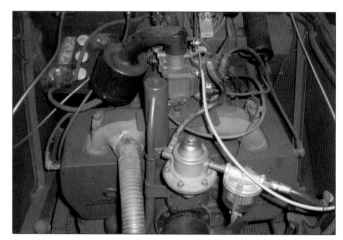

A look at the Pup's engine. *Photo by Michael Banks*

This view of the CT-3 Pup shows its simplicity: canvas fenders, simple stamped steel body, open top and sides, single seat. *Photo by Michael Banks*

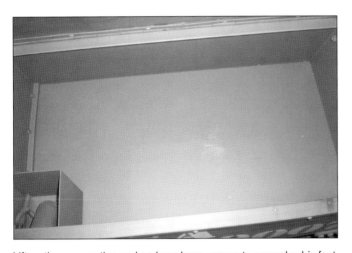

Lift up the rear seating pad and you have access to several cubic feet of storage space. *Photo by Michael Banks*

The Crosley Pup was strictly utilitarian, right down to its heavy (but cheap) canvas fenders. *Photo by Michael Banks*

Another view of the Crosley CT-3 "Pup" as it may have looked during wartime. It would have served best as a fast courier vehicle to get around army posts and airbases. *Photo by John P. Olberholtzer*

Here is a look at another museum-displayed Pup. This one resides at Airborne & Special Operations Museum. Rather than a big cushion in back, this Pup had a rear seat. *Photo by John P. Olberholtzer*

The Crosley "Peep," a miniature automobile built in 1942 by Crosley mechanics for Powel Crosley's young grandson, Lewis L. Crosley. It was probably inspired by the Crosley Pup. The sheet-metal vehicle was powered by two 6-volt car batteries and had a horn and headlights. It was a single-seater, with the steering wheel mounted in the center of the dashboard. The white vinyl-upholstered passenger seat would be removed to access the batteries and the Crosley starter motor that drove it. This photo was taken in 1977, after the mini-car had been restored and repainted. *Banks Collection*

A look "under the hood" of the Peep shows the batteries, motor and chain-and-gear drive that turned the left rear wheel. *Banks Collection*

behind the driver, knees-to-chin. Another version of the Pup had a bench seat in the front, while a cushioned seat and grab bars were mounted on the rear—the same design as used on the Crosley three-wheeled motorcycle. Beneath the seat was about six cubic feet of storage.

Another Pup was delivered to Fort Benning, Georgia, for tests in February 1943. The military ordered 36 Pups in total, and these were delivered to several posts before the end of the year. At least one was built with six wheels. Both Army Ordnance and the Army Air Corps received CT-3 Pups.

After several cycles of tests and changes, the small scout car didn't fulfill the Army's expectations, and no more were ordered. A few were sent to Europe, and some ended up scrapped after the war. Several are known to be in the hands of collectors or on display in museums today.

Crosley, Klotsch and the other engineers had many more ideas for military equipment. Fascinated by tracked vehicles, they decided to build some small-scale versions for specialized tasks, each using the 12-horsepower Waukesha engine. The first idea was the T-28 Snow Vehicle (or Snow Tractor). This vehicle had a small frame housing the engine, which drove and was surrounded by twin cleated tracks. It was as if two pairs of tracks were rolled up side-by-side, the little engine placed inside them and handlebars attached. The handlebars provided steering and a mount for the controls—similar to today's power cultivators. Called the Crosley Snow Tractor, it could pull heavy loads through snow or mud. This was tested and used by the Army in Alaska, and also used by the Army Air Corps.

Next was the Crosley T-30 Tug, a dual-tracked vehicle with a rear seat. It could be used to tow artillery on rough or muddy ground. Four bogie wheels inside the tracks were equipped with rubber tires, so it could be converted to a roadable vehicle. Both front and rear wheels were steerable. A variation of the Tug featuring a cargo area and front seating was dubbed the T-30 20 Track-Laying Mule. It had an optional trailer that also rolled on tracks. There was also a T-30 14 Track-Laying Mule that the Army Air Corps tested.

A six-wheel adaptation of the Tug with larger cleats on the tracks was built for use in snow. It was called the Crosley Snow Tug. Completing this lineup was a Self-Propelled Gun Mount, a low-slung version of the Tug with a seat and a .50 caliber gun. The driver sat upright.

The Crosley T-28 Snow Tractor was little more than an engine surrounded by tracks, with two control arms. The ring at the bottom was for attaching a load to be towed. *Banks Collection*

The Crosley snow-going Tug two vehicle. *Banks Collection*

With the addition of a gun mount, the Crosley Tug became a self-propelled gun. (Note the bumpers with spring mounts.) *Banks Collection*

The Crosley Snow Tug was used mainly as a tow vehicle, but came in several other configurations. It was a higher-profile machine than the Crosley Tug, and had six large wheels to the four smaller wheels on the Crosley Tug. (The Snow Tug also had much larger cleats than the Crosley Tug.) *Banks Collection*

Having no shielding, it didn't look like anything a soldier would want to ride into battle.

The snow-going vehicles, along with Crosley Pups, were sent to the Columbian Glacier in Alaska and to Camp Hale in Colorado for evaluation.

Some Crosley vehicles underwent testing at the Army's Aberdeen Proving Grounds in Maryland. Most Crosley vehicles received positive ratings, but the military didn't order any of them in large quantities. This was in part a matter of the Army preferring to keep things simple by using the Jeep in as many applications as possible, as opposed to trying to field too great a variety of specialized equipment. The Jeep played many roles, most of which required little or no modification.

The Crosley Corporation did better making non-automotive equipment for the military. Before the war ended, it would produce—in addition to the proximity fuze and Mark 14 gunsight—enormous quantities of bomb-release shackles, gun turrets, airplane-tracking radar, field kitchens, radio transmitters and receivers, and both stationary and portable electrical generators.

The Crosley generators—initially a project for the U.S. Navy Bureau of Ships (BuShips)—were powered by a decidedly different kind of engine. Invented by Lloyd Taylor of Taylor Engines in San Francisco, the engine had a block built up from steel stampings. The assembled stampings were brazed together in a high-temperature furnace with a hydrogen atmosphere. The result was an engine block greatly reduced in weight, in comparison with conventional cast-iron blocks. The engine was nicknamed the COBRA, for the COpper BRAzing process used to make it.

It appears that Taylor had submitted a lightweight, six-cylinder engine made with his process to BuShips. The Navy was at the time taking bids for engine-powered generators that could be airlifted to ground troops. Among other jobs, BuShips was responsible for construction and repair, and for engineering, design and development. As such, it was the origin of and entry point for much military technological innovation.

In the course of other military-related work (perhaps the aluminum engine described in a couple of pages), Paul Klotsch became aware of Taylor's engine, discussed it with Taylor and told Crosley about it. Klotsch and Crosley investigated the engine further and Crosley was convinced to buy the rights to the engine and process. The potential for a government contract no doubt figured in his decision. Taylor Engines did not have the resources to go into mass production with the engine, but the Crosley Corporation did, and a deal was made. Crosley hired Taylor to come to Cincinnati as a consultant. He was already thinking about a COBRA-powered automobile.

The Crosley Corporation quickly built six four-cylinder Taylor engines that fit the required specifications and submitted them to the Navy for testing. Each engine/generator unit had to weigh less than 100

The CE-4, a 2-1/2 kilowatt engine/generator set built for the U.S. Navy. *Banks Collection*

A Crosley COBRA engine, set up as a stationary power plant in 2005. *Photo by Michael Banks*

pounds, and be able to run at 5,000 rpm for 50 hours, nonstop. Crosley's engines passed the tests, and the Crosley Corporation got the contract for thousands of engine/generator units to be used as stationary or mobile electrical power plants.

The engine/generator units were used in PT boats, aircraft and anywhere else a lightweight power source was needed. Some were air-droppable. Two models were manufactured for the Navy: CE-2 and CE-4, plus however many variants were made.

There were also two portable versions, one used by

the Army Air Corps. Both were designated CE-5. They were mounted on wheeled platforms, and one was a dual unit. The CE-2 had a 5kw output; the rest were 2-1/2kw.

Crosley's other military engine project was a two-cylinder aluminum engine built for the Army Air Corps. The 20-horsepower engine's task was not to propel aircraft, but to power electrical generators.

Crosley also hired Lloyd Taylor, with an eye toward building a four-cylinder version of Taylor's engine to power automobiles after the war. The Crosley engineering team and Taylor went to work on a four-cylinder,

The Crosley Duck climbing out of the Ohio River at Cincinnati's Public Landing. Left to right: an unidentified U.S. Army captain, Crosley Motors Chief engineer Paul Klotsch and Powel Crosley, Jr. *Banks Collection*

The Crosley Duck carried a total of seven, and could be hooked up to a tracked trailer to carry wounded on litters. *Banks Collection*

44-cubic-inch version of the COBRA engine. Taylor at first wanted to make the crankcase of pressed steel, in order to make the engine even lighter. But Klotsch and Crosley vetoed that idea. Instead, Crosley engineers went with an aluminum crankcase. The final version of the engine developed 26-1/2 horsepower. At 59 pounds, it weighed far less than comparable engines.

Later in the war, Crosley built one final prototype military vehicle: an amphibious, tracked vehicle called the Crosley "Duck." Powered by the COBRA engine, the bathtub-shaped Duck traveled on land or water at will and was large enough to carry seven people. A special trailer—also on tracks—could be hooked up so the jaunty little craft could tow additional passengers or cargo.

Paul Klotsch designed the Duck with the Army in mind, but the war ended before the one-off prototype could be evaluated. The Duck was shown in public only once, on January 8, 1945, when Powel Crosley, Jr., invited reporters and photographers to Cincinnati's Public Landing on the Ohio River to watch it go through its paces.

Crosley, Klotsch and an Army captain rode the craft up and down the shoreline and into the Ohio River as a small crowd watched. The steel-hulled amphibian featured a wooden ship's wheel at the pilot's post amidships. Following the demonstration, the Duck and its trailer joined other Crosley vehicle prototypes in storage. Paul Gorrell has discovered some parts of the vehicle, but the location of the rest of the Duck is unknown.

Powel Crosley, Jr., meeting with military brass during World War II. The Crosley Corporation received several Army-Navy "E" awards for excellence in war production. *Banks Collection*

Crosley's war lineup was kicked off by the Crosley sedan (which he no doubt felt the Army or Navy could use as a staff car) and a modified, open version called the "Mosquito." Two-wheel and three-wheel motorcycles, each powered by the Waukesha twin, were offered to the Army for testing. A miniature Jeep-like vehicle on a Crosley chassis rounded out the offerings. All were powered by the two-cylinder Waukesha. *Banks Collection*

This was the original logo for Crosley Radio from 1922 through World War II. The bolt of electricity through the name was used on just about every Crosley product, as well as the company letterhead, signs, and so on. Naturally it was used as the Crosley automobile logo. *Banks Collection*

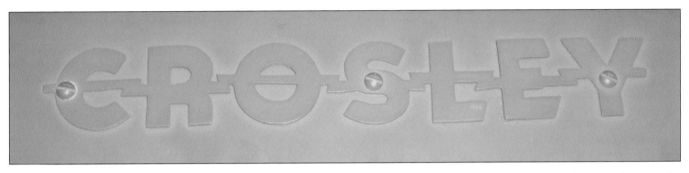

Here is an implementation of the logo as a nameplate on a Crosley CT-3 Pup, painted standard olive-drab, of course. This was placed on the nose of the Pup's hood, as well as beneath the door sill on each side. *Photo by Michael Banks*

"A is for Ample" was an appropriate slogan indeed, as the nation faced shortages of oil, rubber and other vital materials of which the Crosley automobile required less than other cars. This was part of a gasoline ad. *Banks Collection*

CHAPTER 5
1945-1947: A New Start

When the dust settled, Powel Crosley calculated that he had lost $1.5 million building and selling Crosleys before the War. Which is to say, the Crosley Corporation had lost $1.5 million on the Crosley Radio Automotive Division. How much of that was development, and how much was corporate overhead assigned to CRAD is impossible to say. The same is true of losses which may have been shifted from other Crosley divisions for the convenience of accounting.

No matter. By 1944 Powel Crosley, Jr., was deeply involved in planning for renewed auto production. The Crosley-to-be was taking shape on the drawing board. It would be a small car with a small price tag. It would consume little gasoline. It would be, Crosley said, the car for the forgotten man, the man who didn't have a fat wallet, who didn't need a large, showy car to prove something.

Participating in the body design was Carl Sundberg, who had worked with the Crosley Corporation designing radios before the War in addition to styling the Crosley pavilion at the World's Fair. It was rumored that some Hudson designers working on the side contributed to the design. The 1946 Crosley's front end did bear some resemblance to the 1946 Hudson, most especially the standout high nose.

Paul Klotsch directed the engineering details. There were others who weren't credited, as was Powel Crosley's way. Crosley did, however, go to the effort of crediting Sundberg & Ferar as the stylists in an early 1947 ad.

More focused than ever on his automotive dream, Crosley was not looking forward to competing in the post-War domestic product landscape. As he put it, the competition would be a real dogfight, with hundreds of manufacturers who had depended on war production, predictably fighting for the huge consumer goods market that anxiously was awaiting the war's end. At first, perhaps, there would be room for everyone, but soon enough it would come down to battling for survival. He didn't want to be a part of that. With a for-

tune estimated at $20 million, he could settle back and do what he wanted—which was to build automobiles.

Crosley had no illusions about becoming another Chrysler or Ford. His brother, Lewis, had scouted the field and discussed matters with industry heavyweights, men like his golfing partner, George Mason, chairman of Nash-Kelvinator (later American Motors), and Joseph and Robert Graham, of Graham-Paige. What these men had to say convinced Lewis that there was no chance of competing with the Big Three. Lewis carried the message to Powel, who nevertheless felt that he could find a place in the market. A gradual buildup to selling 150,000 units per year would be quite satisfactory.

Aware that extending his involvement in automaking would stretch his most important asset—himself—too thin, Crosley decided to divest himself of his interest the Crosley Corporation. But he would do it on his terms. He would hold on to the Cincinnati Reds and WLW. WLW was an institution. Crosley Broadcasting was still at the leading edge of broadcast technology, and still a leader in programming and marketing. Using the call letters WLWT, Crosley Broadcasting would soon be setting the pace in television programming. Perhaps most importantly, WLW was something of a family heirloom for Powel Crosley, Jr. Less than a quarter-century earlier he had taken his first tentative steps into broadcasting, a hopeful hobbyist who was uncertain as to exactly where this radio thing might take him. As it happened, it just went up and up, and took Crosley Radio and Powel Crosley's fortunes with it.

With news of the Crosley Corporation being on the market, E.L. Cord's Aviation Corporation (AVCO), a staggeringly large conglomerate (rather like Paramount today) was eager to buy. But there was a catch: AVCO wanted WLW. Already a giant in shipbuilding, airplane manufacturing and so many other industries that *Time* called it "Everything, Inc.," AVCO wanted to get into broadcasting in a big way. The prospect of parting with WLW might have been a deal-breaker had Crosley's accountants not informed him of the huge tax debt he would incur if he kept WLW while selling the Crosley Corporation. Given the circumstances Crosley chose to sell. In a complicated mix of cash and stock trades, Crosley picked up over $15 million and a directorship with AVCO while retaining a place on the board of the Crosley Corporation. And he kept the Cincinnati Reds.

The sale would be up for stockholder approval in November. Confident that the deal would go through, Powel Crosley, Jr., incorporated Crosley Motors in August 1945. Ever-conservative and tight-fisted, he sold stock in the venture to insure that he would not be risking much of his own money. Over a half-million shares went quickly at $6 a share, with Powel Crosley controlling 60 percent.

That September an optimistic Powel Crosley, Jr., told reporters that he expected cars to be coming off the line at the rate of 125 per day by December, with deliveries to dealers to begin in January 1946. But there was a big problem: The Crosley plant in Richmond was included in the sale to AVCO. This meant that the newly-minted Crosley Motors had no place for its assembly line.

The fact that Crosley was willing to announce that production would commence less than ninety days in the future probably says something about his state of mind at this point. He also announced that the Crosley would have an all-aluminum body. (That never came to pass.) Getting into production so quickly implied that the design and tooling were finalized, and that contracts had been signed with suppliers. But none of that really mattered because Crosley Motors had neither a factory nor a workforce to build the Crosley. Maybe the statement was simply a way to generate more excitement about the new car.

Crosley searched Cincinnati and its suburbs for a suitable factory building. Most of the available facilities were too small or too large, and Crosley was outbid on the one factory that would have been perfect. Extending his search farther afield, he decided on a factory in Marion, Indiana, a town about 50 miles north-northeast of Indianapolis, and 120 miles from Cincinnati.

The 170,000-square-foot building was used by Peerless of America to manufacture refrigeration parts during the war, and—appropriately—had been the site of the Indiana Motor Truck Company from 1909 through 1932. Crosley Motors paid $350,000 for the site. Crosley COBRA engines and front axles for the car would be manufactured at a small plant in Cincinnati—one of two buildings that Crosley retained in the AVCO deal.

Body stampings would come from the Murray Body Company in nearby Indianapolis. A plethora of other parts would journey by truck and rail from suppliers throughout the Midwest.

Start-up costs soon ripped through the three million Crosley raised. Once again there was not enough money to go into production. But this time Crosley had an easy solution. He merely peeled off a million dollars from his personal bankroll and lent it to the company—secured with $200,000 notes payable on set dates beginning in 1949.

Delays in tooling and a machinists' strike at the Cincinnati engine plant put off the Marion plant's startup. Finally, on May 9, 1946, the first Crosley automobile (a sedan) came off the line. By July 4 the line had produced just 149 cars, but the pace was increasing. There were problems, but nothing that couldn't be fixed. For example, the first 500 units went out without Crosley emblems because the supplier was late delivering them. "Crosley" was painted on the bumpers in red. Most got their badges later.

The new Crosley automobile was decidedly different. Its flat-sided, streamlined look was like nothing else on the market. It has been said that the flat sides resulted from Crosley having a certain amount removed on each side, so that the cars could ride side-by-side in railroad boxcars. For the same reason, door handles were higher on one side than the other. The more cars he could pack into a railroad car, the cheaper it was to ship them.

The car looked to be a bit larger than its predecessor. Feedback (and jokes) from the public must have convinced Crosley that a bigger small car was needed. The design began with the same 80-inch wheelbase and 40-inch track as in 1939. 12-inch wheels (painted "Chinese Red," just like the prewar Crosleys) were once again used. But the overall length of the sedan was 145 inches, while the width was 49 inches—longer, yet slightly narrower than the old Crosley, which measured 120 inches by 53 inches. In comparison, the 1946 Ford DeLuxe sedan had a 114-inch wheelbase and was 196.2 inches long by 70.9 inches wide.

That same 1946 Ford, which cost just under $1,200, was of course a slightly-redone 1942 model, as were all the cars from mainstream automakers. Crosley hoped that new styling and a new kind of engine would give him a jump on the competition. But novelty was not all he was relying on to get attention. A brand-new Crosley cost the same as an eight year-old used car; Crosley hoped to pull in a significant percentage of used-car shoppers who might become enamored of the idea of buying a *new* car, instead. Gasoline was still rationed and here was the Crosley with gas mileage at least twice that of any of the major makes. Crosley made use of this fact from the beginning with advertising that bragged on the Crosley's economy. "Weighing about one-third as much and operating for half as much as other so-called light cars," went one slogan. "HIGH POWER, light weight, low cost and economy in operation," said another.

Economy in construction was important from the very beginning. Hence the sliding windows (no crank mechanism). Only one tail light was provided, though customers could specify the second light as an option when they ordered a Crosley, or add an aftermarket light. There were no hood ornaments on Crosley CCs early on. Nor were there ornamental moldings or trim. Simple door hinges that showed on the outside were cheaper than hidden hinges. The Crosley had only one external door lock. This was on the passenger side; the driver could lock his door from the inside and climb out the passenger door. Front parking lights were inside the headlights, which were not sealed-beam lamps. (Later in the CC series Crosley Motors would add small parking lights underneath the headlamps.) Everything possible, from door handles to bumpers, wiper blades and the glove box, seemed to be miniature versions of normal automobile equipment.

A major cost-saving measure was to eliminate external trunk access. The space at the rear was tiny, anyway, so Crosley made it accessible from behind the rear seat—just like early Nash Metropolitans, but with less space. No trunk lid meant no hinges, no costly fabrication and no extra assembly.

Crosley Motors' assembly plant in Marion, Indiana. It began life as a truck factory, and then made refrigeration equipment during World War II. *Banks Collection*

The first postwar Crosley was a slab-sided, streamlined sedan with a snub nose. Compared with the prewar Crosley, it was a greatly simplified design. The prewar model's high nose was retained, with less of a drop from the windshield. The windshield itself was a conventional split type, raked back at a sharper angle. It featured wipers on both sides. The sliding-glass side windows were carried over, along with the external vents (common in autos of the era). Large, fixed windows were installed for rear passengers. All Crosleys were two-door models; there were no four-doors. *Banks Collection*

A 1946 Crosley sedan outside the Marion, Indiana, assembly plant. Headlights on the new model were set into tunnels between the nose and the quarter panels. A low, small grille opening was retained. In place of fenders were sweeping quarter panels that were front-and-rear mirror images of one another. The steeply-sloped rear end met the up-curving quarter panel at the back bumper. A difference in angles of the curves of the turret top and the rear deck gave the car a hump-backed look. Its appearance earned the nicknames "roundside" and "bull nose." (Note that there is no badge on this Crosley. The emblem supplier didn't deliver them until after production was underway. Cars with missing nameplates went out with "Crosley" painted on their rear bumpers.) *Banks Collection*

A well-restored 1947 Crosley CC convertible, more than 60 years after it was assembled in Marion, Indiana. As is obvious, the convertible was a twin of the sedan. The top rolled back on hardwood cant rails to rest just above the Crosley "T" emblem in the rear. As can be seen with this model, bumperettes were optional, as was a second tail light. *Photo courtesy of Jim Bollman*

Crosley Motors' Chief Engineer Paul Klotsch (L) talks with Powel Crosley, Jr., next to a 1947 Crosley at Pinecroft, the Crosley estate in Cincinnati. *Banks Collection*

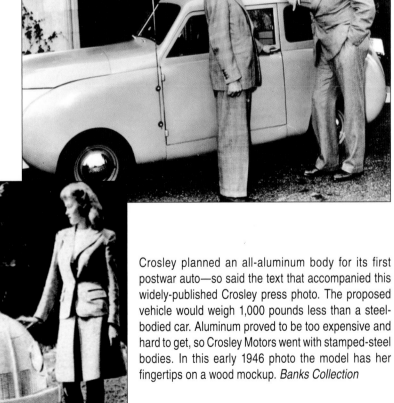

Crosley planned an all-aluminum body for its first postwar auto—so said the text that accompanied this widely-published Crosley press photo. The proposed vehicle would weigh 1,000 pounds less than a steel-bodied car. Aluminum proved to be too expensive and hard to get, so Crosley Motors went with stamped-steel bodies. In this early 1946 photo the model has her fingertips on a wood mockup. *Banks Collection*

CROSLEY

Crosley Motors could not use the Crosley "radio wave" logo because it was still property of the Crosley Corporation (now AVCO). It was replaced with this "Indian Arrowhead" logo. One theory has it that it was inspired by the Trans-World Airlines logo, which had an arrow through it; Powel Crosley was on TWA's board of directors. The logo appeared on the faces of gauges, hubcaps and elsewhere. The letters were slanted to suggest speed. *Banks Collection*

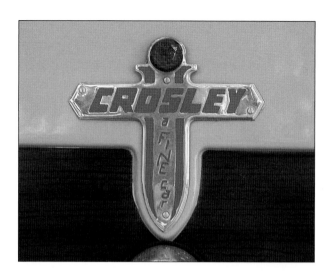

The nameplate or emblem for the postwar Crosley. It carries the little auto's most enduring motto: "Crosley – A Fine Car." The cross-shape is a play on "Cros" in "Crosley." The background is Crosley's favorite "Chinese Red" color. (He frequently used this red on his aircraft, as well as on the wheels of Crosley autos.) The emblem eventually appeared on the noses of all Crosley vehicles. It was also used on the tailgates of later CC-series Crosley Pick-up trucks, the rear doors of wagons and the backs of sedans and convertibles. The emblem in this photo is mounted on the rear door of a Crosley Station Wagon. The "jewel" set into the ornament came in two colors: red for the rear, and clear for the front. *Photo by Michael Banks*

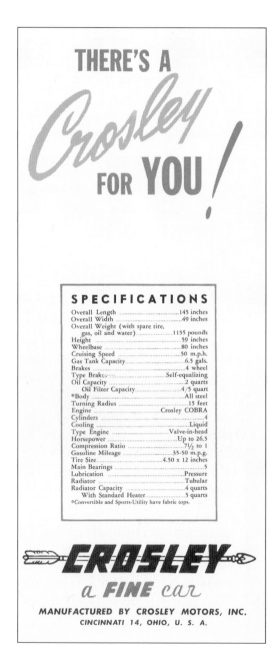

THERE'S A

Crosley

FOR **YOU**!

SPECIFICATIONS

Overall Length	145 inches
Overall Width	49 inches
Overall Weight (with spare tire, gas, oil and water)	1155 pounds
Height	59 inches
Wheelbase	80 inches
Cruising Speed	50 m.p.h.
Gas Tank Capacity	6.5 gals.
Brakes	4 wheel
Type Brakes	Self-equalizing
Oil Capacity	2 quarts
Oil Filter Capacity	4/5 quart
*Body	All steel
Turning Radius	15 feet
Engine	Crosley COBRA
Cylinders	4
Cooling	Liquid
Type Engine	Valve-in-head
Horsepower	Up to 26.5
Compression Ratio	7½ to 1
Gasoline Mileage	35-50 m.p.g.
Tire Size	4.50 x 12 inches
Main Bearings	5
Lubrication	Pressure
Radiator	Tubular
Radiator Capacity	4 quarts
With Standard Heater	5 quarts
*Convertible and Sports-Utility have fabric tops.	

CROSLEY

a **FINE** *car*

MANUFACTURED BY CROSLEY MOTORS, INC.
CINCINNATI 14, OHIO, U. S. A.

The motto, "Crosley: A Fine Car" began showing up at the end of 1947. (It was literally written "a FINE car.") It was a rather pedestrian motto for Crosley, whose slogans were usually more lively or dramatic. *Banks Collection*

The export version of the Crosley automobile was called the "Crosmobile" to avoid it being confused with the "Crossley," a British car. Crosmobiles were distinguished from Crosleys by the name appearing on emblems and gauges. Where the destination country required it, Crosmobiles were built as right-hand drive cars. The phrase "a FINE car" was omitted from the badge, probably to avoid the cost involved in translating the phrase and problems fitting some translations into the available space. *Banks Collection*

The box chassis beneath the new Crosley was about the same size as the prewar model, but had a sturdier, more straightforward look.
Photo courtesy of Jim Bollman

As noted, the promised aluminum body never materialized. Apparently, though, Powel Crosley was hoping to put out an aluminum-bodied car as late as spring of 1947. That, or he just wanted to explain away the mess. A lengthy advertisement in April informed readers that, "The early production of Crosley cars will be built with all steel bodies, due to the difficulty of obtaining, handling, drawing and forming of available aluminum sheet. The change is due, also, to the delays that have resulted, as well as the very much higher cost of aluminum sheet plus the large amount of waste occasioned by the deep drawing of aluminum."

An alternative explanation for the talk of aluminum bodies may have had something to do with competition. In 1945, Chevrolet began planning a small car called the "Cadet." Designed to appeal to Crosley's market, it was intended to sell for under $1,000. Its light weight, smaller engine and technologically advanced design would have made it economical to operate—even though the Cadet was larger than the Crosley CC. It

weighed a full ton and had a 108-inch wheelbase. The Cadet project was quietly shut down in 1947 when GM bigwigs realized that every Cadet they sold meant that a larger, more profitable model did not sell. Ford quashed a similar project—a car based on a vehicle Ford was already manufacturing in Germany—for the same reason.

Had these cars gone into production, Crosley would have been out of business by 1949, at the latest. The fact that Ford and GM didn't build their compact cars strongly implies that they didn't consider Crosley worth competing against. (Chrysler had already had a flirtation with small, low-cost autos in the 1930s, with their "Star Car," a dream car that didn't materialize. When word got out that Ford and GM were thinking small, Chrysler made a small detour in that direction with something called the "Wayfarer.")

While the looks of the new Crosley were as striking as the fact that it was even available, for many the radical, lightweight COBRA engine was the main point of interest. The COBRA was developed by Californian Lloyd Taylor and presented to the United States Navy as a power plant for air-droppable, stationary electrical generators, among other uses.

This lightweight engine was built using ideas no one had ever tried. Instead of being a heavy, cast-iron block, the COBRA's block was assembled from 125 steel stampings. The cylinder walls were made with chrome-molybdenum steel tubing only one-sixteenth of an inch thick, which promised to eliminate hot spots and facilitate even operation. The pistons were cast aluminum. Cylinder bore was 2-1/2 inches, and the stroke 2-1/4 inches. Total displacement was 44 cubic inches (721cc).

When the pieces were put together, they were crimped or press-fitted to stay in place. Pure copper was melted into the joints between the parts, welding them in place. Then the assembly was brazed. (Hence the name: COpper BRAzed.) Hydrogen brazing was used, which involved placing the block in a roller hearth furnace with a neutral atmosphere. Lindberg Engineering of Chicago manufactured the hydrogen furnace, and got a lot of publicity out of it, distributing a booklet that detailed how the Crosley COBRA block was made.

The COBRA was water-cooled, and was protected from rust inside the water jacket by a coating of hard plastic. It seemed invulnerable to damage from freezing—in one test, Crosley froze a COBRA engine block filled with water, to prove that freezing could not damage it. Not directly; a running engine could still overheat if the water inside was frozen and thus unable to circulate and carry away heat. Owners would have to remember to add anti-freeze in the winter.

COBRA engines of a slightly different nature were used to power electrical generators in PT boats, tank turrets and aboard ships, and in other field equipment. They were also used as "starter motors" for B-17 and B-24 bomber engines.

The military version used a 9:1 compression ratio and high-octane gas, and ran at 5,600 rpm. The automotive version ran at 5,200 rpm, with a 7.8:1 compression ratio. It used regular leaded gasoline. The high rpm and high compression helped the small package (often cited as "not much larger than a typewriting machine") put out relatively high horsepower for its weight. As used in the Crosley automobile, the COBRA was a valve-in-head engine with a single overhead cam and one single-barrel carburetor. It developed 26-1/2 horsepower, over twice the old Crosley's power.

Powel Crosley holds a COBRA engine block with its valve cover and cast-aluminum crankcase in his lap in this publicity shot. He would have struggled to do the same with a conventional engine block. Stripped down like this, the COBRA weighed just 59 pounds. The block by itself weighed only 14 pounds. The complete engine was 133 pounds. *Banks Collection*

Crosley's COBRA engine represented an entirely new approach to building the basic structure of an engine. Instead of being cast in one piece, the COBRA block was made of 125 steel stampings and pieces of steel tubing, which were copper-welded and then brazed together in a high-temperature furnace. The transmission is mounted to the engine in this 1946 factory photo. *Banks Collection*

The logo designed for the COBRA engine. *Banks Collection*

A Crosley COBRA engine *in situ*, just as it was installed in the factory in 1947. Owner Bill Angert had the block treated to eliminate its vulnerability to electrolysis, using technology that wasn't available in the 1940s. *Photo by Bill Angert*

Crosley Motors chief engineer Paul Klotsch spoke about the new Crosley before the Society of Automotive Engineers (SAE). He explained that the car might indeed get up to 50 miles per gallon—at 30 miles per hour. This apparently was not exciting enough for advertising. Before the car went into production, Crosley Motors claimed that it had a top speed of a mile a minute, and would get 50 miles per gallon at 30 or 35 miles per hour. Over the next several months the Crosley's performance mysteriously improved—at least on paper. A top speed of 65 and then 70 miles per hour was claimed, as was the car's ability to wring 50 miles out of a gallon of gasoline no matter what its speed. When the car reached the market, the claims were dialed back to 50 miles per hour and "36 to 50 miles per gallon." The recommended cruising speed dropped from 50 to 40 miles per hour.

Even if the Crosley couldn't do 70 on level ground, the company held that it was a zippy little car. An interesting cartoon in a Crosley Motors newspaper ad showed a Crosley sedan beating a big, anonymous American sedan in an impromptu drag race on a city street. It was captioned, "POWER: flashes out front in the pick-up."

Crosley offered three models of his "car for the forgotten man" for 1946. The assembly line ran sedans initially, then mixed in convertibles. Both were four-passenger models, and the sedan weighed 1,150 pounds (the convertible, a little less). Crosley might have liked to have claimed the Crosley was a five-passenger car, but no one would have believed him—not with it being narrower than the prewar model. So he settled for

"plenty of leg room inside for four huskies" like himself.

The earliest of these CC models had no door panels. When added, the interiors were either brown, or a darker brown called "pigskin." A circular cluster of gauges faced the driver from the vertical dash: oil pressure, water temperature, fuel gauge and generator charging indicator. To the right was a round speedometer with odometer. There were spaces on the passenger side of the dash for an optional radio, speaker and ashtray. The heater was also optional. ("The forgotten man" was tough.)

The headliner seems to have been a paper-based material, and the rearview mirror was small. A tiny, unornamented horn button, rubber floor mats, and small gas, brake and clutch pedals completed the interior.

A look at the CC's minimalist interior. Upholstery in this restored Crosley is similar to the original—brown simulated pigskin. The ashtray, radio and speaker were options. Headlight dimmer switch is on the floor, between the brake and clutch. Notice the tiny door handles. *Photo courtesy Jim Bollman*

An optional Crosley radio, proudly bearing the new Crosley Motors arrow logo. It was manufactured by Motorola. Perhaps Powel Crosley wanted to keep Crosley Motors separate from the Crosley Corporation in all respects. (Zenith also manufactured some receivers for Crosley automobiles.) *Photo courtesy Jim Bollman*

The convertible had a "roll-back" top. (Crosley Motors called it their "Jiffy Rig.") A double layer of weatherproofed fabric in beige slid back on hardwood rails to tuck in at the belt line above the rear deck. It was likely an improvement over the folding top. (Nash would use the same top on its later 1940s Rambler convertibles.) Interior lining was brown. DeLuxe versions of the sedan and convertible offered washable simulated pigskin upholstery and interior lining. Optional exterior colors were Island Green and Gem Blue.

A quarter-ton pickup truck, referred to simply as "the Crosley Pick-up Truck," completed the lineup. Some customers said that it could carry as much as 750 pounds. It shared the standard Crosley chassis with the cars, and the body except for the rear half. The roof over the cab was steel, unlike prewar pick-ups. Early pick-ups had no door panels. Eventually cardboard was used, itself textured or covered with a simulated leather-grain material.

The earliest Crosley Pick-up trucks were roundsides. Most pickups had a narrower back bumper. Red wheels indicate manufacture in 1946 or 1947. *Photo by Bill Angert*

This Crosley convertible has a special clear top, one of three that the owner made. (One of the others was opaque fabric, while the third was solid.) The front "T" emblem, with the correct clear jewel, can be seen, as can the hood ornament. The car has the optional bumperettes. *Photo by Michael Banks*

The later 1947 Crosley pickup trucks got a new rear-end treatment, to match the squared-off shape of the station wagon. As shown here, the truck also shared the stamped side panels of the station wagon. There was no rear bumper. *Photo courtesy Jim Bollman*

National advertising for the Crosley automobile was mostly confined to small display ads in the low-cost back pages of magazines. These were the same pages in which Crosley had advertised his Model T self-steerer and the miracle Gaso-Tonic 30 years earlier. On rare occasions large color ads would run in important publications like *The Saturday Evening Post*. But most ads were the same 2-, or 3-inch by 6-inch, lightly illustrated display ads that spoke of Crosley's personal pride in the car, often carrying his likeness in addition to that of one or more Crosley vehicles. The ads brought home the point that the Crosley was cheaper to buy and operate than any other car in America. The mantra of "50mph/50mpg" was frequent.

Accompanied by a small portrait and his signature, Crosley's earliest ads began with this quote: "For 35 years it has been my dream to build a fine, light car. Here it is—smart, fast, economical." He packed an incredible amount of information into the space that followed. The Crosley was modern and streamlined. The Crosley was big, in all but weight and price. The four big huskies and their baggage rode with ease. The amazing COpper BRAzed engine was lightweight and delivered stunning power. It was revolutionary...nothing like it in 40 years...a *fine* car that would go 60 miles an hour while delivering 50 miles per gallon...

Sometimes the ads turned deficiencies into advantages. The car was narrow? Why, that meant it took up less room on the road, and was thus less likely to sideswipe another vehicle. It was easier to maneuver, too, for ease of parking and darting out of danger. Drivers of large cars would automatically exercise more caution around a Crosley. And because of its light weight the Crosley would *give* in an accident, making damage less likely.

Powel Crosley packed even more into his brochures. He seemed to share a basic tenet with David Ogilvy ("The Father of Advertising") who maintained that someone interested in a product will read everything there is to read about it; Crosley often took off on themes. For example, he claimed a variety of aircraft features for his car, just as he had before the War. The Crosley, he declared, had a "rakish aircraft heritage" and "four deep aircraft type seats." The standard color was "Duv-Gray," which was "reminiscent of the wings of a mourning dove." The rear seat was "copied from the luxury equipment of airplanes designed to sell for

The 1947 interior was about as basic as it could be, although this one has an aftermarket radio and speaker. The small horn button identifies this as an early model, and the rubber floor mats are pretty much like what came with the car. There is no lining on the doors. *Photo courtesy of Jim Bollman*

Here is a look at Powel Crosley's "airplane-style" bucket seats. The upholstery is faux-pigskin and the padding is a bit thin, especially on the seat backs. *Photo courtesy of Jim Bollman*

$50,000 and up." The Crosley's overall "Aircraft Flavor" was described thus in a 1946 Crosley Motors brochure:

"It's only natural that Mr. Powel Crosley, Jr., director of TWA and owner of several private planes, should make the car that bears his name 'the nearest thing to flying on wheels'! Even the seats are the 'pilot-type'; there are smart, aircraft-style sliding windows that really *control* air circulation; the instrument panel suggests a modern aircraft; the exclusive Duv-Gray coloring blends with the 'wide blue yonder'! In riding comfort, too, this great *fine* Crosley car is plane-like. It virtually *glides* along, and you're scarcely conscious of its speed. Set it on its course, and it practically drives itself."
Just add wings.

Aviation was a major preoccupation of the public in the 1920s and 1930s. Just as in the 1910s with automobiles, anyone who set or broke a record for altitude, speed or the shortest elapsed time between two cities was lauded by the news media, sometimes as a hero. (Witness Charles Lindbergh and Amelia Earhart.) Powel Crosley, Jr., as noted in an earlier chapter, had been in the aviation industry more than once, and had owned

several landmark aircraft. He also had used airplanes extensively in promoting Crosley Radio and WLW. Given all this, it was natural that Crosley would do all he could to connect his new automobile with the glamour of aviation.

At least two Crosleys *did* fly, in a circumstance similar to that of the Crosley Pup tested by the Marine Corps in 1942. On August 23, 1946, two sedans were loaded into a DC-3 at Cincinnati's Lunken Airport, then flown to La Guardia Field in New York. From there they were driven to Macy's Department Store. On August 27, the first day the cars were displayed, 9,000 people viewed them. According to the *New York Times*, 1,000 shoppers were ready to buy, but the store could not sell more than its quota of ten Crosleys per day. At that, delivery would not be until October. Compared to other makes, this wasn't a long wait; many Big Three buyers had to wait a full year. The price was $853.58, plus local sales tax.

By this time Crosley Motors had 600 dealers and orders for 30,000 cars. Powel Crosley's frustration must have been intense. Over $24 million in orders, and he was having trouble getting more than two or three cars to each dealer. Total production for 1946 was 5,007, bearing serial numbers CC46-100 through CC46-5205. This was comprised of 4,987 sedans, 12 convertibles and 8 pick-up trucks. Crosley Motors was never in danger

Macy's Department Store once again welcomed the Crosley automobile to its sales floor. The ad spoke of speeds up to 65 miles per hour, of hauling four husky adults and of low operating costs. Images hinted at the Crosley's "airplane-like" qualities, and illustrated how it could beat big cars off the line. The car drew a crowd of 9,000 admirers that first day—but it could sell only ten cars a day. *Banks Collection*

of exceeding its WPA-assigned quota of 16,000.

In general, the Crosley was well-received, particularly in newspapers and magazines that tracked the latest trends in things automotive. The novelty of being the first new car since 1942 brought the Crosley a lot of glowing press. *Time* and *Newsweek* gave detailed reports on the car before it went into production. *Popular Mechanics* liked it enough to run a photo of its christening. *Popular Science* found the car praiseworthy, and detailed its specs—next to a Crosley-provided photo of what the editors thought was an aluminum body. The COBRA engine got as much attention as the car itself, mostly in trade journals but all positive. At the other end of the scale, *Consumer Reports* limited itself to this terse comment on the CC46: "Substandard comfort and resale value. Not acceptable."

Mechanix Illustrated's Tom McCahill summed up

the Crosley's lack of comfort with this statement in his July 1947 test report: "…in my opinion the only time you could cruise in a Crosley at 50 miles an hour and still be comfortable, would be if you were sitting in one that was loaded on a fast freight train which was doing 50 miles an hour." He would find Crosley's later Hot Shot and Farm-O-Road more to his liking.

It really was a rough-riding little car, but how much comfort could one expect at such a low price? As for resale value, Powel Crosley's comment was, "The lower the original price of a car, the less it will lose in resale value."

Already adept at the rules of export and foreign marketing—and having established a worldwide network of distributors with the Crosley Radio Corporation—Powel Crosley, Jr., found few barriers to selling his cars as Crosmobiles in Canada, Europe, South America and Asia. Existing Crosley appliance distributors did most

CROSMOBILE

Your Best Xmas Buy!

PRICES FROM $1090

ALL MODELS JUST ARRIVED

THE MANAGEMENT AND STAFF WISH ALL OUR FRIENDS THE HAPPIEST HOLIDAY GREETINGS

NIPPON AMERICAN AUTOMOBILE CO., LTD.

ON "B" AVE ONE BLOCK SOUTH OF 10TH ST. TEL. (43) 6824 (43) 0826

The Nippon American Automobile Co., Ltd., in Tokyo was a major distributor of Crosley automobiles in Japan. There may also have been a Crosley dealer in Osaka. American servicemen as well as Japanese citizens bought Crosmobiles here. *Image courtesy of Jim Bollman*

of the marketing, each being well-established and aware of who could or could not sell automobiles. The newest Crosleys were shown every year at the European auto show in Brussels, and dealers in Austria, Belgium, Denmark (with offices in Germany), England, France (price: 59,500 Francs) and elsewhere were signed up. There was also a dealer in Johannesburg, South Africa.

A Japanese company called Nippon American Automobile Company was formed to sell the Crosley in the Far East. The same or another company sold Crosleys in the Philippines.

Crosley Radio had done extensive business in Latin-American countries before World War II, and Crosley Broadcasting was in the process of building a high-power shortwave broadcast network in South America when World War II began. Now, however, there were trade restrictions on automobiles. It seemed that Mexico (and other Latin-American nations) required that cars be at least assembled in a country with which certain trade agreements were already in place.

This was not an unusual requirement. Early in his career, Henry Ford had run into similar requirements in countries like Australia. Since prohibitive customs duties were levied on completed automobiles but not on parts, Ford shipped knocked-down cars to be assembled in the countries where they were to be sold. Crosley did the same thing for cars bound for distributors or Central America, South America and the Caribbean. He shipped knocked-down cars to Mexico. There, they were assembled by a company called *Distribuidora Au-*

tomotriz Crosley, SA, which shipped them on to dealers in Argentina, Brazil, Colombia, Cuba, Honduras, Mexico, Puerto Rico and Uruguay. Some countries had more than one Crosley distributor.

In addition to the aforementioned countries, Crosley CCs and CDs were seen in Angola, the Antilles, China, Mozambique, Norway and Switzerland. Used Crosleys were sometimes offered for sale in the Japan and European editions of *Stars & Stripes* by servicemen returning to the U.S.

There are no numbers for foreign production or export. Presumably assembled machines for export as well as the parts for knocked-down cars to be assembled in Mexico were included in Crosley's overall production figures. All indications are that Crosley Motors continued exporting complete cars and parts right up to July 1952.

The 1947 models—serial numbers CC47-10000 through CC47-26999 and CC-2700 through CC-31999—were in dealerships by December 1946. The sedan and convertible looked just like the 1946 models. This made little difference to car-shoppers. Shortages and rationing added extra luster to "new." And the Crosley was the only all-new car, excepting the 1947 Studebaker Starlight. By the end of the model year, Crosley Motors would sell more than five times as many 1947s as it had 1946 models.

Sedans once again led the way in production, with 14,090 built. (The OPA had initially set the ceiling price of the sedan at $749, but it soon was raised to $849.)

Convertibles trailed behind at 4,005, followed closely by trucks, 3,183 of which went out the door. The lowest seller for 1947 was a new vehicle, also introduced in December 1946: an all-steel station wagon. Without the momentum of an immediately preceding model year, it sold just 1,249 units. That would change.

The new Crosley wagon was very different from Crosley's prewar station wagon. In addition to carrying the new post-War front end, it had flat sides with panels stamped in. And it was the first all-steel station wagon, which made it different from all other wagons. Other manufacturers were still building their station wagon bodies with wood, in whole or in part. Crosley Motors could advertise the wagon as sturdier ("no wood to rot") and lighter. Even so, fake wood appliqué (also referred to as "inserts") was added to panels on the rear sides, to give the Crosley wagon the look of a woody. This was inspired by the fact that wood had been used on station wagons for so long that the look, at least, was expected. Besides, it looked good. It was available in blonde, maple or walnut. Later, a wicker pattern would be added to the choices.

The two-door wagon included one of Crosley's favorite elements, a removable rear seat. The rear side windows followed the extended rear end nearly all the way back to the angled C pillar, and they were sliding windows that passengers could open, just like the windows in the doors. The rear end was sharply distinct from the sedans and convertibles. It was angled forward from the bottom to the top. (This look was resurrected in AMC's Gremlin in the 1970s.) The slant made the car look longer than it was. Clamshell rear doors opened into the cargo space. By virtue of being small, having two passenger doors and being all-steel, the Crosley station wagon got a lot of publicity.

Not incidentally, the pick-up truck received a new rear-end treatment. The sides of the bed dropped the "roundsides" shape and took on the flat look of the station wagon sides. At the extreme rear the bed slanted forward, from the bottom to the belt line. This meant that the wagon and pick-up used the same side stampings below the belt line, just as they used the same front body stampings—another money-saving tactic.

The all-steel Crosley station wagon beat Plymouth's steel wagon by a year, and it would catch on quickly. The rear side panels were shared with the pickup truck, which saved money on body stampings. The small CC hood ornament is easy to make out in this photo. Note the optional outside mirror and dual windshield wipers. *Photo courtesy of Jim Bollman*

Just as the station wagon was based on the pick-up truck, so a panel delivery truck could be based on the wagon. Omit the hole for the side windows and the station wagon side-stampings became panel delivery stampings. Using the wagon's clamshell doors at the rear also saved money. Both the wagon and the panel truck kept their spare tires underneath the rear. *Photo by Bill Angert*

This rare full-page 1947 Crosley Motors advertisement from *The Saturday Evening Post* shows each of the new Crosleys in color. The station wagon has fake wood-grain siding. "No wood to rot, swell, shrink or rattle," the ad boasts. The sedan is presented once again as having "aircraft flavor" styling. The convertible was Crosley's attempt at a sporty car. Low operating costs are emphasized for the work vehicles—a pick-up truck and panel delivery. Heater, radio, a second brake light and turn signals were still optional. The ad itself cost close to $30,000. *Banks Collection*

The ConvAIRCAR was a fiberglass-bodied automobile that was powered by a Crosley COBRA—the automobile part, that is. Strap-on wings and a high-power Lycoming aircraft engine provided air power. *Banks Collection*

These little Crosley Motors magazine advertisements were among Crosley Motors' first, appearing in January and March of 1947. The same and similar tiny ads appeared in *Time, The New Yorker, Popular Mechanics, Popular Science, The American Magazine, Life, Colliers, The Saturday Evening Post, Science Illustrated, Newsweek, Factory Management and Maintenance* and many other publications. The tone is "one man to another," and the ads are jam-packed with facts. They advise the reader that the gas mileage is super, the car is streamlined, it costs less than anything else on the road, it has "aircraft flavor" and it can still carry those four big huskies Crosley liked to pack into his autos. The next advertising campaign would offer testimonials by Crosley owners as to gas mileage and other performance elements. *Banks Collection*

Times were good. During the first fiscal quarter of 1947, Crosley Motors earned $309,563 on sales of $5,485,894, and sales were doing nothing but going up. Production passed 100 cars per day, but more capacity was needed. To meet demand, Crosley Motors increased the size of the engine factory by 21 percent. Later in the year a new addition increased the Marion plant's final assembly area by 40 percent. The latter alone cost the company $450,000.

The engine plant expansion was critical because of sharp increases in demands for the COBRA. Thousands of engines had to be supplied for Crosley automobiles, of course, and to satisfy the government contract for portable generator units. Those engines were intended to be used for a limited time period and then replaced, which made for a self-renewing market. The COBRA was also in demand by thousands to fulfill all sorts of power requirements. Word had gotten out about the

COBRA and lots of people had ideas to put it to work. Before long the demand would more than double the engine plant's work force to 700. Employment at the Marion assembly plant would approach 1,200.

A marine version of the engine was developed by John Peek, and along with it a new 44-cubic-inch class for hydroplane racing. A COBRA-powered hydroplane could do almost 90 miles per hour, and it quickly caught on. Another interesting application for the COBRA was in a flying car put together by Consolidated Vultee (soon to become Convair) in 1947. The ConvAIRCAR consisted of a lightweight auto and detachable wings and a Lycoming aircraft engine and propeller. The car was fitted out with both automobile and airplane controls. The fiberglass automotive component—which was about the size of a Crosley—was powered by a Crosley COBRA engine.

Two were built and successfully road-tested and flown. However, one crashed when the pilot confused the automotive gas gauge with the aviation fuel indicator and ran out of gas. Of course the crash had nothing to do with the COBRA, but the ConvAIRCAR development program was cancelled.

The COBRA had temporary success in the Mooney Mite. The Mite was a single-place airplane designed by Al W. Mooney as a low-cost sport plane. It had a 27-ft. wingspan, was 18 feet long and weighed only 415 pounds. Perhaps because he was like Crosley in enjoying building things differently, and because he liked to save money, Al Mooney decided to cast about for an engine for the Mite other than the usual Lycoming or

The U.S. Forest Service's "Mechanical Mule" was custom built around a Crosley COBRA engine, transmission and differential. It could haul 1,000 pounds. It was three feet wide and had a 5-foot turning radius—perfect for getting around wilderness trails. *Banks Collection*

Continental power plants used in aircraft of the day. The right engine would help maintain the airplane's light weight and superior performance. He asked several industrial and automotive engine builders, among them Waukesha, to participate, but none got involved.

When Mooney visited Powel Crosley in Cincinnati, Crosley was enthusiastic. Mooney decided to try the COBRA engine as its power plant. The Mooney Mite flew with the COBRA engine for the first time in May 1947. It performed well, flying at 100 miles per hour and getting 400 miles out of its 8-gallon fuel tank.

But there were problems. Exhaust valve wear caused power losses. The load on the front main bearings proved excessive, and was bending the crankshaft. (Lateral pressure from the wide drive belt was responsible.) By then, Mooney related, "Crosley was having service problems of their own. Their cooperation diminished as Powel became less enchanted with aviation. Finally they made a change in their crankshaft, which put us back on page one again."

The engine finally passed its Aircraft Type Certification and received FAA clearance in July 1948. Then, the seventh Mooney Mite delivered to a dealer suffered a broken crankshaft in flight. The plane landed safely, but that was it for the Crosley COBRA powering an airplane. Mooney replaced the COBRAs with 65-horsepower Lycoming engines and there were no more problems. And it turned out that Lycomings cost less than the Crosleys.

Ironically, Powel Crosley's Crosley Aircraft had developed a four-cylinder, air-cooled airplane engine called the Cobra in 1930. It was patented and certified, but never put into production.

The U.S. Forest Service developed a carryall vehicle they called the Mechanical Mule, based on the COBRA engine. The vehicle consisted of a single-axle tractor and single-axle trailer that was only 36 inches wide and which had a turning radius of five feet. It was perfect for trail-building and fire-fighting. Using COBRA engines, plus Crosley drive trains, the Forest Service built at least ten Mechanical Mules in their Portland, Oregon, Regional Equipment Laboratory in 1949.

Yet another COBRA-powered vehicle was the Gasporter, a small fuel tanker designed for use at airports or to fuel fleets of cars on lots. It was built on a Crosley chassis, but manufactured by Engineering Research Associates of St. Paul, Minnesota. An unknown number were built.

The Gasporter, a mobile fuel storage tank for airplanes or automobile parking lots. Built on a Crosley chassis and powered by the COBRA engine the Gasporter was particularly popular at small airports. With a capacity of 200 gallons, the Gasporter could be used to fuel, defuel and transfer fuel between aircraft at 25 gallons per minute. *Photo courtesy of Jim Bollman*

A straight-on look at the 1947 Crosley CC shows how narrow the car was. The prominent nose, descended from the prewar models, is emphasized by the dorsal fin. Compared with the rest of the car, the bumperettes seem outsized. *Banks Collection*

From the side, the nose is also prominent, reminiscent of some prewar Hudson or Graham automobiles. (Or, for that matter, the 1946 Studebaker Skyway Champion.) In general, the lines are balanced and the car doesn't seem as small as it really is—especially if one imagines it with 15-inch wheels. *Banks Collection*

CHAPTER 6
1948-1949: Flying High

In November 1947 *Time* magazine referred to Powel Crosley, Jr., as "the big man (6 feet, 4 inches) with the midget car." Although Crosley hated his car being called a "midget," he was no doubt delighted with the short article about the new 1948 Crosley models. "Among them," *Time* noted, "is the cheapest postwar model he has yet produced: a two-passenger multi-purpose sports and general utility car."

The Sports-Utility Vehicle, as Crosley called it, was, at $799, priced lower than any other Crosley. Although Powel Crosley didn't nickname it the "SUV," he can be credited with coining the term. This vehicle was very like Crosley's prewar Covered Wagon.

The Sports-Utility Vehicle was a mixture of the Crosley pickup truck and station wagon. It used the truck's drop-down tailgate and the station wagon's sides, along with the front end, chassis and engine from the 1947 model CC. The entire roof was removable canvas, as were the rear sides, upper back and passenger doors—held on with snap fasteners and straps. The elimination of so much steel, plus the omission of the rear seat, helped make the low price possible.

An early flyer for the Sports-Utility Vehicle targeted sports- and businessmen alike: "Pile in your gun cases… give the dogs a boost and you are off for the narrow lanes where the game birds fly. Drop the fabric sides and you are protected against the hardest storm. Or, equip your delivery department with Crosley Sports-Utilities and watch service costs go down. Traffic jams will not strand your Crosley…crowded curbs will not keep your Crosley circling the block."

Although the Sports-Utility Vehicle would get its share of attention, by far the most popular Crosley model for 1948 would be the station wagon. It was initially priced at $929, though manufacturing costs soon drove it up to $1,032, then $1,096. In all, 23,489 wagons were built—more than by any other manufacturer in the world. Many buyers probably came to Crosley dealers because they were persuaded by lower purchase and operating costs, and were swayed in the direction of the wagon by the fact that the sedans and convertibles had almost zero trunk space.

The Sports-Utility Vehicle was Powel Crosley's big news for 1948. It was marketed as a vehicle that could go hunting or fishing as easily as it could be driven around town. Only two of Crosley's "big huskies" fit into this model because it didn't come with a rear seat, although one could be ordered at extra cost. The 500-pound cargo compartment could be opened to the air by rolling up the canvas sides. Or, the entire top and sides could be removed, leaving one with a convertible pickup truck much like the prewar Crosley pickup truck. The doors were also canvas and held in place by snap fasteners. *Photo courtesy Jim Bollman*

Crosley's Sports-Utility Vehicle without its canvas top, side and doors. The bow supports were also removable. Although no provisions were made for off-road travel, the floor pan was flatter than that of other Crosley models. Powel Crosley had hopes that the cost of labor and materials would drop enough so that he could produce a slightly altered version for only $500. Although it was advertised for off-road use, it did not have four-wheel drive—just the standard two-wheel, three-speed drive train used by all Crosleys. *Banks Collection*

The new Crosley station wagon featured flat sides and fake wood panels. It was the first all-steel wagon made in the United States. *Banks Collection*

Tom Miller's partially-restored 1948 Crosley station wagon has the hood ornament and small bubble running lights that were added later in the model year. It also has an optional radio—note the antenna. Yet another extra is the decorative chrome trim running along the belt line. As this photo shows, the horn was tucked in just under the front bumper. *Photo by Michael Banks*

The demand for station wagon bodies increased so rapidly during 1948 that the Murray Body Company couldn't keep up with it. Crosley Motors was fortunate to find another body maker to supply station wagon roofs, sides and oil pans. This was the Gerstenslager Company, located in Wooster, Ohio. Gerstenslager was founded as a carriage-maker in 1860. The company started building specialty truck bodies in the 1920s and ultimately became noted for building custom mobile units for hospitals, remote broadcast units for television stations and other manner of specialized vehicles, including postal-service trucks. In postwar years it became particularly well-known as a manufacturer of bookmobiles. (As of 2011, a Crosley oil pan serves as a cover for a sanding machine at the plant, an artifact of the days when the Crosley wagon was a big seller.)

Because Gerstenslager was three times farther from Marion than was Murray, shipping was higher. Crosley Motors passed the extra cost along to its customers.

Prices still were low on the other Crosley CDs. Powel Crosley was constantly seeking ways to keep all the models' prices below $1,000; he badly wanted to use that as a marketing point. The sedan and convertible prices were set at $1,039. The panel delivery started at $975, and the pickup at $950. But there was little he could do to keep the wagon's price from climbing to

$1,096, and still retain profit margins.

All Crosley models underwent a minor cosmetic change in 1948. From then through 1952 the wheels would be off-white instead of what had become the standard red. Red wheels were originally intended to build brand recognition (much in the way daytime running lights were used by GM in the 1990s). Why the change? Red paint may have cost more. Or perhaps the decision to change was based on esthetics. Serial numbers for the 1948 model year ran from 1948 CC-32000 to CC-61256.

Production for the 1948 model year: 23,489 station wagons, 2,836 trucks (including pickups, sedan deliveries and Sports-Utilities), 2,760 sedans and 2,485 convertibles, for a grand total of 31,570. Most of these numbers were well below those of 1947—in the case of the sedan, appallingly lower. Even with their numbers combined the rest of the 1948 Crosleys didn't come anywhere the station wagon's 23,489 in sales. Obviously, Crosley Motors had done something right with the station wagons. The question of the hour was, "What can we do to make the other cars and trucks sell like the station wagon?"

Advertising increased. In 1948 Crosley Motors ads appeared in *Popular Science*, *The New Yorker*, *Life*, *Time*, *The American Magazine*, *Collier's*, *Newsweek* and of course *Popular Mechanics*, among other magazines. (According to Powel Crosley, *Popular Mechanics* always had generated the most orders in his automobile accessories days.) But the ads were still the small, black-and-white kind. While seeming to save money these ads cost Crosley in the long run. They just didn't give the Crosley the *oomph* and legitimacy of a half- or full-page color ad like those of the Detroit automakers. To many readers, the ads made Crosley Motors look like a much smaller operation than it was—like it might be just another transient company that was too ill-financed to hang tight in the market. And the ads weren't large enough to be memorable. Whenever he was asked about them, Powel Crosley uttered the same cryptic response: "Small car, small ads."

Did he really believe that statement had any practical meaning? Or was the low-cost advertising more a reflection of his tight-fistedness? Conversely, he certainly showed no reluctance in spending money to advertise in the radio business. Crosley Radio routinely ran full-page ads and hired celebrities to endorse its products. (Musicians and singers usually were shown with Crosley products, although he once actually had evangelist

Sister Aimee Semple McPherson pose for publicity photos with a Shelvador refrigerator.) Nothing like those successful advertising campaigns was being tried by Crosley Motors.

In July 1948, a new series of ads appeared, headed, "Crosley Now Has That New Look." The new look was in the form of three pieces of hardware added to the front end: two large, wing-like louvers and a conical "spinner" that was, the ads said, "adapted from aircraft propellers." (The conical hub over the center of an airplane propeller is called a "spinner.") The cross- or T-shaped front emblem was not included on Crosleys with the louvers and spinner.

The cosmetically altered cars were called "1948-1/2 models." For those owners of early 1948 models who felt left out, a bolt-on update kit was available from Crosley dealers. A few owners of 1946 and 1947 CCs added the louvers and spinner, too. Then they drove around and collected looks from people who thought they'd bought a new car.

Interestingly, "that New Look" was a catch phrase that originally gained currency in women's fashion advertising, beginning in 1947. By 1948 "that New Look" was used to describe anything different—in fashion, home and office décor, amusement rides, railroad engines and a wide variety of other products. It appears that Powel Crosley may have picked up on the popu-

This New Jersey Crosley dealer believed in advertising on the go. The dealer put a Crosley sedan delivery right to work as a parts car, customer ferry, and road emergency car. Note the single tail light on this 1948 CC model. The spare tire peeking out at the rear would normally be hidden by the sedan delivery's bumper, which for some reason has been removed. This vehicle also shows the clamshell-style rear doors, and the similarity between the sedan delivery and the station wagon. *Photo courtesy of Crosley Automobile Club*

In mid-1948 Crosley Motors tried something original: a 1948-1/2 Crosley with a "new look." It may have been the first-ever midyear model from an automaker. (Detroit would use the idea later, with, among others, the 1953-1/2 Rambler Custom Cross-Country Wagon, and the 1964-1/2 Ford Mustang.) The new look involved a front-end treatment that consisted of two radiator louvers and a bullet shape that Crosley described as a "gleaming spinner derived from aircraft propellers." The wing-like louvers were initially painted to match the car body, but the factory soon switched them over to chrome. Viewed straight-on, the accouterments made the car look awkward. *Banks Collection*

Here is a Crosley wagon with the "half-year" upgrade, minus one of the wings. The grille is painted the body color, indicating that this was an early 1948-1/2. The change in appearance was radical, to say the least. *Photo courtesy of Karl Schultz*

larity of the phrase and exploited it to his own ends.

The idea behind this clever move was to generate "new model" excitement and kick up sales without the expense and poor timing of actually bringing out a new model. Inspired by slow sedan and convertible sales, the new front end may have helped, but it was still the station wagon that took the lion's share of sales. And thanks to the wagon 1948 would be Crosley Motors' best year.

For some years after World War II Japanese companies were rather informal in their recognition of international copyright and trademarks. This tendency showed up in the country's nascent postwar automobile industry in the form of "knock-offs" of automobile designs from other countries. The Crosley was a victim of this in March 1948 when Nissan introduced a car it called the "Datsun DB." As can be seen in the accompanying image, it was almost a duplicate of the Crosley sedan.

Sad to say that, like the Crosley in the U.S., the Datsun DB was the first automobile in Japan to have a new look. It just wasn't Datsun's look. The DB was based on a Datsun truck with a wheelbase that was just over an inch shorter than the Crosley's. The engine, a 15-horsepower four-cylinder, was strictly Datsun.

Some reports say that Powel Crosley, Jr., was enraged when he found out about this. He no doubt protested to his Japanese distributor, his congressman and the State Department. He may have tried to wield some back-channel influence through his cousin, an admiral in the U.S. Navy. By 1949, Nissan had changed the design of the car's front and renamed it the DB-2. The Japanese

In 1947, Japanese automaker Nissan obtained a Crosley sedan. They took it apart and studied it, much the way Powel Crosley, Jr. disassembled and studied a competitor's refrigerator design 15 years earlier, and then figured out a better way to build it. Nissan simply copied the Crosley's design and put it on their own chassis. They called the car the Datsun-DB and put it on the market in March 1948. When Powel Crosley learned about it, he was angry but no direct action could be taken, considering the fact that the occupying forces were working to get the Japanese economy back to a productive state. In 1949, however, the design was quietly changed. *Image courtesy of Alan Bent*

design diverged from the American thereafter.

Crosley engineers were already hard at work on the 1949 models. They would differ from the 1946-'48 CC models in many respects, beginning with the body styling. Crosley Motors no longer could get by on being small, economical and funny-looking. Detroit manufacturers finally had gotten up to speed and were creating their own excitement with all-new models, among them cars like the landmark 1949 Ford. People were becoming as accustomed to seeing the Crosley as they had been to the slightly-changed Ford, GM and Chrysler postwar models. Crosley no longer had its "only new car on the market" cachet, either.

On top of everything else, the fear over gasoline prices and rationing that had in part driven Crosley sales was gone. Given that, auto shoppers found the size, power and *newness* of the products rolling out of Detroit alluring. The war was over, and it was time to enjoy life. Crosley Motors desperately needed an all-new 1949 model with its own allure to answer Detroit. It might have to add something special, to boot.

There was no question that Crosley Motors would have to compete with Detroit. Outwardly Crosley liked to tell the press that he considered himself to be competing for the used-car market, that he was no threat

to GM, Ford or Chrysler. He told *Time* magazine, "I should like to make clear that our ambitions . . . are comparatively unpretentious."

Any money that the public was planning to spend on automobiles was potentially new-car money, and a new car was a new car. And although Powel Crosley, Jr., knew Alfred Sloan and Henry Ford, II, personally, Crosley was the competition. The giants were merciless against competition, be it Studebaker, Willys, Crosley or one another.

The 1949 Crosleys—officially designated the CD series—missed the usual fall rollout for new models; they were presented to the public in mid-December at New York's Park Lane Hotel. The new car *was* different, with a body style that was more like those of the mainline makes than any Crosleys before them. Up front, the Crosley CD had an undistinguished hood ornament and a new emblem, a crest based on Powel Crosley's family coat of arms. The high nose persisted, making plenty of room for the emblem. (Serial numbers for the 1949 model year ran from CD-100001 to CD-108628.)

Beneath the nose, the grille was composed of three chrome-plated louvers that resembled wings. They reminded one of the 1947 Chevrolet Fleetline, and even more of the 1946 Hudson Commodore Six—or the 1946 Ford.

Gone was any hint of the slab-sided CC. The new Crosley had standard-looking integral front fenders. They were rounded at the top, and cut toward the rear

The new Crosley emblem was based on the Crosley family crest, which Powel Crosley had paid to have researched to its origins in England. *Photo by Bill Angert*

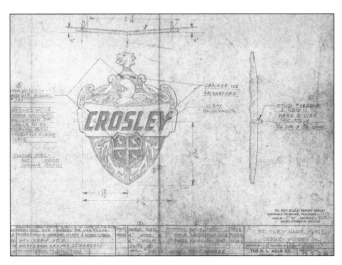

Blueprint for the new Crosley emblem, manufactured by the D.L. Auld Company of Columbus, Ohio. *Banks Collection*

with the grille as they dipped down from the headlights.

Above and forward of the front wheel wells, "bump outs" or character lines were creased into the fenders to offer an illusion of width. (These were also called "strakes" and "speedlines.") Sliding-glass door windows were retained in the sedan, convertible, sedan delivery and pickup. The station wagon not only had sliding door windows, but also sliding side windows for back seat passengers. Fixed rear side windows were included in the passenger cars. The fresh air vents that sat just ahead of the doors were larger.

The rear fenders on sedans and convertibles had double character lines above and in front of the wheel wells. The lower line was a horizontal crease with a sharply-angled vertical component that angled back toward the well from the door, to suggest speed. (The front character line had the same vertical component.) The upper line was a swooping arc, continuing the acute

The 1949 CD grille, along with traditional fenders, gave the Crosley a more mainstream look than it had ever had. The fact that the cross-pieces look like wings is no accident. Powel Crosley's obsession with airplane-like features was still strong. *Banks Collection*

The 1949 Crosley station wagon demonstrating that it was big enough for a small family. This one has the blonde wood treatment. *Banks Collection*

angle from the lower vertical line in an organic curve. It, too, provided the visual cues of a wider fender and speed. The tops of the rear fenders on the sedan and convertible grew from behind the B-pillars to form rounded semi-fins, previewing the 1950s "battle of the fins." The gas filler was moved from the side to the top of the driver-side fender. Of the hump-backed look of the CC sedans there was no hint. The rear end, as seen from the side, was squared-off. The car had dual tail lights/turn signals—at no extra charge. (The first CD station wagons and pickup trucks had single taillights, however, until the supply left over from the preceding year ran out.)

The car looked larger, though it wasn't. Being narrower made it look longer. Crosley brochures pushed the "big" theme with phrases like "The Large Look" and "The new Crosley is big!" The brochures noted also that the Crosley still carried those same "four big huskies" with ease. It was obvious that Powel Crosley, Jr., was well aware of what America really wanted, but still *hoped* that America would want his car. In fact, he was confident that Americans would fall in love with his car—if only he could get their attention long enough. Slogans like "The car America needs" and "The car America has been waiting for" sounded good, but as it would turn out Crosley could not make them true. The unfortunate truth was that the car America was waiting for was hitting the highways with a 114-inch wheelbase, a big V-8 engine and lots of chrome.

From the side, the rear end of the Crosley sedan and convertible were squared off. Both models came with stationary rear side windows. *Banks Collection*

This photo clearly shows the character lines on the front and rear fenders. They suggested a wider car, to go along with the advertising line that the new Crosley was "big," even though it was narrower than its predecessor. Only the doors were unchanged, made with the same stamping dies used to make the CC's doors. A new crest and small ornament adorned the high hood. *Banks Collection*

A rear view of the 1949 Crosley shows just how narrow (49 inches) it was. But it had a full complement of lights—dual running/brake/turn-signal lights, and a license plate lamp. Clean lines finished the fenders. Optional bumperettes enhanced the relatively narrow bumper, and posed no problems with the trunk lid because there was no trunk lid. A wide rear window made driving safer. *Banks Collection*

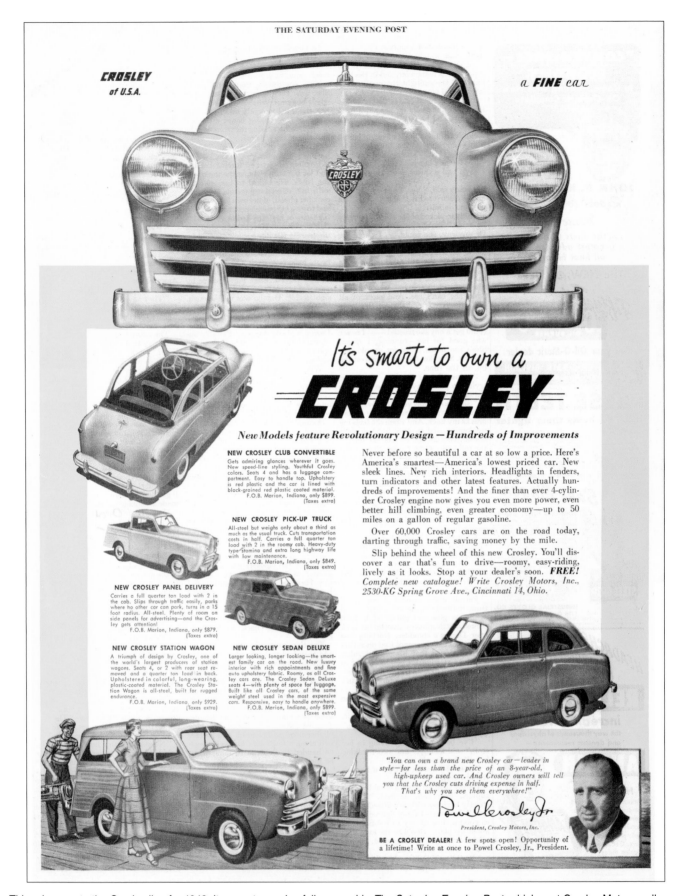

This ad presents the Crosley line for 1949. It was a two-color, full-page ad in *The Saturday Evening Post*, which cost Crosley Motors well over $20,000. Powel Crosley was out to capture the public's attention in a big way. "It's smart to own a Crosley," "You see them everywhere" and "Larger looking, longer looking" were the latest slogans. *Banks Collection*

The new Crosley had a rectangular gauge cluster: speedometer, odometer, ammeter, fuel gauge, engine water temperature and oil pressure. However, to save money, the early production CD pickups, sedan deliveries and station wagons had left-over round gauges from the CCs installed, to save money. Crosley probably figured that the dashboard's looks were less important to buyers of these vehicles. The remainder of the dashboard was unchanged. *Photo by Michael Banks*

In an unusual move, Crosley Motors co-advertised with Borg-Warner, which manufactured clutches for Crosleys. Crosley Radio had often co-advertised with companies that made complementary products—batteries, networks, DuMont Television, and some suppliers. This particular ad was a home run: it was a full-page ad that put a color photo of a Crosley wagon in front of millions of magazine readers, while strongly associating Crosley with Borg-Warner's name and quality reputation. The ad appeared in *Newsweek, The Saturday Evening Post* and other magazines. *Banks Collection*

The convertible was now the "New Crosley Club Convertible." Tops were black, although for an extra charge one could obtain a tan top with red trim. As with the 1948 model year, the top slid back on hardwood-lined cant rails. The spare tire—still an option—was mounted beneath the rear of all CDs. *Banks Collection*

Crosley Motors' sedan was renamed the "Crosley Sedan Deluxe." One emphasis was on the "rich auto upholstery fabric" now used in the sedan and convertible. *Banks Collection*

The 1949 Crosley pickup truck used the CC-style bed and doors with the CD front end. This one has a contemporary two-tone paint job. Painting the rear panels of wagons and pickups in colors that contrasted with the main body color was always popular. *Photo courtesy of Clyde Haehnle*

Some pickup trucks came out of the factory painted one color. The paint job gave them a foreshortened look, or at least made the bed look much smaller. *Banks Collection*

Panel delivery trucks were also offered in a single color. The 1948 panel delivery had CC doors and rear end, with a CD front. *Banks Collection*

Like the pickup truck, Crosley's station wagon and panel delivery were marriages of 1948 rear and 1949 front. One big difference for 1949 was an optional full-height, vertical rear door that was hinged on the left side. (The clamshell-style doors were still available.) This door could be ordered for both wagon and panel delivery. *Banks Collection*

A look through the open door into the back of the Crosley panel delivery truck. Painted the same inside and out, and with the gas filler tube out in the open, this is about as stark as a commercial vehicle might get. It probably came with a rubber floor mat, but the jack may have been optional. *Photo by Bill Angert*

The Crosley's size made it a natural for comedy. Crosley wagons were big in the amusement business, as rolling billboards and particularly as "clown cars" in circuses. Wagons also showed up in comedy movies, as in this scene from *Africa Screams* (1949) which starred Bud Abbott and Lou Costello. A prewar Crosley Parkway Delivery was used in another Abbott & Costello film, *Abbott and Costello in Hollywood* (1945). Other comedies in which Crosley autos appeared include *The Noose Hangs High*, *Three Ring Circus*, *Animal House*, *Porky's II* and a Laurel & Hardy war bond newsreel. *Photo and information courtesy Crosley Automobile Club*

There still was no trunk lid on the sedan or convertible, but they were nice-looking cars. Not as streamlined or fancy as, say, the Nash Airflite, but more than acceptable. Many of the little touches that were left out of the Crosley in the past—things that people expected in an automobile—were there. In addition to everything else, the wheel covers were given attention: flatter hubcaps were phased in because the previous high-domed wheel covers extended beyond the edge of the car's body and could strike curbs. In typical Crosley fashion, the earlier hubcaps were used up first.

As ever, the CD had some really different features. For one, the Crosley's six-inch, riveted mechanical shoe brakes were replaced in May 1949 by the first disc brakes—hydraulic, at that—to be used on an automobile. Disc brakes were installed on all four wheels. (It was not until September that Chrysler announced it would make disc brakes standard on its Crown Imperial model.) Sometimes called "pinch brakes," or "spot brakes" because the brake pads were small circles, the braking system was manufactured by Goodyear-Hawley—"Hawley" being Jesse Hawley, who invented the floating-lining brake system used on the first 1939 Crosleys.

Goodyear-Hawley disc brakes were a new attraction for the CDs. They were designed by Jesse Hawley, who had invented the floating-lining brakes used in the 1939 Crosleys. Disc brakes had seen use in aircraft landing gear so naturally Crosley wanted them for his car. It was another "airplane-type" component he could list. By this time, "airplane-type is better" seems to have been his motto. The brakes used rather small pads: they were circles, about an inch in diameter. But they worked. (A woman at Crosley Motors' Cincinnati ad agency dreamed up the trade name "Hydradisc" for the brakes. Powel Crosley refused to believe that a woman could have thought up the name. What, he asked, could a woman know about the workings of automobiles? She was probably inspired by the "Cobra" engine.) *Courtesy of Crosley Automobile Club*

As marked an improvement as the airplane-type brakes may have been, Crosley Motors outfitted the early-production CD models with six-inch shoe-type brakes left over from the CCs. Times were tough, and saving money was vital. Nothing was wasted. The stamping plates for the CC's doors were reused, so that doors from 1946 through 1949, and even 1950, could be used in a Crosley of any year. At certain points, only five leaves were used in leaf springs on the passenger side of the car, while six were used on the driver's side, where more support was needed most of the time.

Just as Crosley was introducing the first automotive disc brakes, trouble came from another Crosley innovation: the much-praised COBRA engine. While the engine had proven to be very reliable at constant speeds for long periods during military tests, it behaved differently under the varying speed and load conditions encountered in daily road use. Its tolerance for heat was very low, compared with conventional automobile engines. If coolant ran low, there was likely to be warping, with loss of power and other problems.

Equally disastrous was the development of pinhole leaks in thousands of COBRA blocks, which brought in a flood of complaints. The plastic internal liner broke down and interaction between the salt-based anti-freeze in common use at the time and the COBRA's various metals produced electrolysis, which led to tiny holes in the block. (One mechanic reported that a customer drove into a dealership with dozens of toothpicks plugging the holes in his engine.) This caused coolant to drain away and contaminate engine oil.

A genius at engines and unconventional design, Paul Klotsch developed an engine with a cast-iron block that otherwise had the same specifications as the COBRA. To save time and money the new engine used most of the same parts as the COBRA—except for the block, of course. Klotsch also took the opportunity of the redesign in added improvements like valve rotators, which decreased wear and tear. The new engine was called the CIBA (for "cast-iron block assembly").

Production on the new engine started as soon as possible at Crosley Motors' Cincinnati engine plant, probably near the end of 1948. Amazingly, it has been reported that the company continued to install completed, leak-prone COBRA engines until the supply was exhausted, just as it had done with their leftover hubcaps and brake shoes.

The supply of COBRAS must have lasted through January 23, 1949. A factory letter to dealers only, dated February 3, 1949, stated that all Crosleys would come with the new CIBA engine beginning January 24, 1949. The public announcement was not made until several weeks later.

The new Klotsch engine would turn out to be a real champion, in more ways than one. Still, Crosley Motors faced a dilemma. Something like 50,000 COBRA engines had been installed in Crosley automobiles. Additionally, an unknown number were sold for other uses, such as powering electrical generators, refrigeration

Crosley Motors replaced the COBRA's radical "tin block" design with the more conventional cast-iron block CIBA. The engine's design would outlast Crosley Motors by two decades. Hundreds of CIBAs (if not several thousand) are in use today. *Banks Collection*

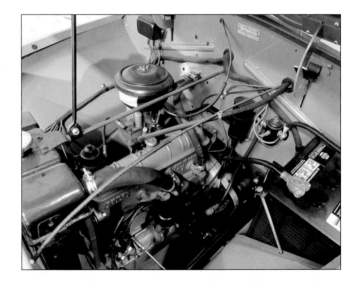

A look at the CIBA under the hood of a Crosley CD sedan delivery. Everything is easily accessible—battery, spark plugs, coil, voltage regulator, distributor, belt, oil and radiator fillers, carburetor and air cleaner. This promoted cleanliness, and made oil leaks and other problems easy to spot. *Photo by Bill Angert*

units on trailers and railroad cars, and air-conditioning systems on buses.

There was no government-ordered recall as would happen today, but Crosley Motors did replace thousands—if not tens of thousands—of engines in customer cars. The move was voluntary on Crosley Motors' part (refusing to address the problem would have been suicide for the company, and may have gotten the government involved). So, it may have been limited to cars under warranty. Nor did the company pay the total cost for engines it did replace. Advertisements and mailings announced that Crosley owners could exchange their old engines for new cast-iron block engines for the price of $89 per unit, including federal tax and freight. The ads noted that the cost of removal and installation (about 5 hours' labor) would be borne by the car owner. (There is no word on whether adjustments were made on non-automotive engines. Since the engines sold to the government were planned to have a limited lifespan, the electrolysis problem probably made little difference in the big picture.)

Was $89 enough to cover materials, manufacturing, handling and shipping for each engine replaced? The rebuilds could have been done at a profit. Undoubtedly some customers forced the company to replace their engines for nothing, but Crosley motors was unlikely to have planned the replacements so as to lose money. So, the expense of setting up a separate line to rebuild engines at the factory may not have been devastating. And one can't help but wonder: How many of those COBRA engines that came in were quickly examined, disassembled enough to remove and replace the block, and then sent back out with the same old working but worn parts as they'd come in with? The Crosleys did like to save money wherever they could.

Direct costs aside, the loss in goodwill and sales was incalculable. Powel Crosley was later to remark, "It was those damned [COBRA] engines that killed us." The damage to the Crosley's reputation was enough to dissuade untold numbers of new-car buyers from choosing Crosley.

Still, the company didn't exactly go broke. Sales of around $25 million for the fiscal year ending in July 1949 assured that. But the net profit of less than $1.5 million surely was not what it might have been.

There are COBRA engines still running today, powering vehicles and stationary devices. Over the years the owners must have been very careful about water level and lubrication, and those in temperate climes prob-

ably drained them during cold weather rather than risk using an anti-freeze that might break down the water jacket lining.

The CIBA took the place of the COBRA in all commercial engine applications. Crosley continued to supply the military with electrical generator units, using the CIBA. CIBAs were sold as marine engines (and set quite a few records). Transitier used them in forklifts, and Totemaster powered its factory material-handling flatbeds with CIBAs. Crosley made its own material-handling vehicle, the Crosley Tug, which could pull loaded trailers around factories or airports. Manufacturers of amusement park vehicles and rides used the CIBA to power their creations. Specialty manufacturers modified any number of Crosley cars and pickup trucks to look like fire engines or railroad trains. Some of the fire trucks pulled ladder trailers, with seating for more child riders.

Dazzling new technology, catchy slogans and uncommon designs had not driven Crosley Motors to the forefront of the automotive world. And now sales were slumping. As he had done since his radio days, Powel Crosley, Jr., responded to company troubles with changes in management. In particular, he hired top regional sales managers from Kaiser-Frazer to replace his existing sales executives.

Then, to help America (and perhaps himself) forget about the COBRA disaster, he put something special on the road: a sporty, two-seat roadster that was like nothing made in America. He called it the Crosley Hotshot, introducing it at a hotel reception in New York on July 13, 1949. It was on display at Macy's and Fine Cars, Inc., the next day.

It had been two decades since American automakers had produced roadsters on a regular basis. They had last been popular in the 1920s, when Americans bought over 300,000 of them. Dodge had introduced its D-29 Wayfarer roadster in 1948 for the 1949 model year, but the Wayfarer was in a different class. On a 115-inch wheelbase with a 230.2-cid straight six that generated 103 horsepower, it was not a small car. To be sure, it was a two-seater and a drop-top, but a vehicle of its size could hardly hug the road on turns. It weighed over three times the Hotshot's weight of 1,000 pounds, and cost twice as much.

The Hotshot was given the Crosley Motors series designation "VC." Serial numbers for 1949 models were VC-10001 to VC-10727. Crosley was enthusiastic in his announcement of the roadster, proclaiming that,

This is how Crosley Motors presented the Hotshot, as a lightweight, sporty car with special appeal for the young and "young at heart." The factory photo emphasizes leisure. But always willing to take any buyers he could get, Powel Crosley also put forth the idea that the Hotshot could be a one- or two-person family car for daily use. *Banks Collection*

Here is a good example of a well-kept Crosley Hotshot, owned by Karl Schultz of Ohio for more than 40 years. He has done major mechanical work on the car as well as regular maintenance. He also repainted it. Karl put this car together using parts from a wrecked Crosley Super Sports and a Hotshot body he found in a creek bed. *Photo courtesy of Karl Schultz*

with the Richmond plant's capacity of 4,500 cars per month, Crosley Motors could easily turn out 10,000 Hotshots by the end of the year. Such was the demand he anticipated.

Powered by the 26-1/2-horsepower CIBA engine mounted behind the front axle, the Hotshot had an 85-inch wheelbase and a cradle frame—higher at the ends than in the middle. With 7 inches of ground clearance it was unlikely to roll over. Rear suspension was combined leaf- and coil-spring, and all four wheels had hydraulic shock absorbers. The car weighed about 1,000 pounds, and was of course outfitted with the new Hydradisc brakes. It hugged the road on curves.

The transmission had three speeds forward and one reverse. The gearshift was rooted in the transmission hump far beneath the dashboard. The shaft rose a few inches on a slant, then angled sharply back for about a foot before rising another few inches to the grip. It was possible for someone with a large hand to suffer skin abrasion as shifting action jammed a knuckle or two into the ignition key—which is exactly what happened to journalist Tom McCahill when he test-drove the Hotshot for *Mechanix Illustrated*.

Just as the prewar Crosleys did, the Hotshot had a high windshield plenum and a single-piece windshield. The top was fabric, with separate side-curtains, like those of several European cars, including the 1950s Triumph TR series. The top did not fold up like those

on prewar Crosleys. The owner had to assemble the top in place. It was stashed in the small space behind the seats. The seats themselves were simple buckets, the kind Crosley liked to call "airplane-type." They were less than comfortable on long drives.

Passenger doors were little more than decorative tokens that filled in the small opening by each seat. It was probably easier to get into and out of the car without them. They were easily detached, and optional. Radio, heater and ashtray were also optional. A spare tire mount was installed on the rear deck at the factory, but the spare wheel with tire was optional.

The Crosley high nose continued with the Hotshot, although it dipped downward in front at a steeper angle than in other models, and did not end in a grille. The new Crosley emblem resided proudly at headlight level. The headlights themselves were housed in prominent pods that stood high in the gentle dips between fenders and hood. The headlight pods were available in red or black, to contrast with the car's color.

A distinctive feature of the Hotshot was that it was designed to be stripped down for racing. Bumpers, spare tire, fabric top and supports, front running lights, tail lights, headlights and windshield were made to be removed, which took 104 pounds off the car's weight. *Life* magazine, of all sources, vetted a speed of 73 miles per hour for the car, unstripped. The magazine further noted that souping up the engine would punch up the

Here's the first page of the four-page Hotshot brochure. It lures the reader in with what just might be a scene on an untamed European mountain road. The page also introduces the rest of the Crosley lineup. The artwork in this brochure was by Count Alexis de Sakhnoffsky. *Banks Collection*

This page of the Hotshot brochure offers the car's specifications and details the benefits of the CIBA engine and Hydradisc brakes. It also stresses the dual personality of the Hotshot, how it can perform as a road or a track racer, and even excel at hill-climbing. *Banks Collection*

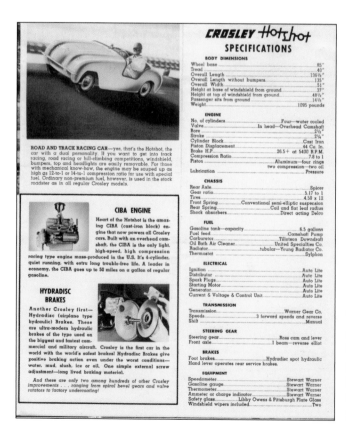

top speed to 84 miles per hour. England's *Autocar* magazine thought the Hotshot significant enough to warrant coverage. It reported that with a 9:1 compression ratio and using 100-octane fuel, the CIBA developed 36 horsepower at 5,600 rpm. It noted that the CIBA normally used a 7.8 to 1 compression ratio, which could be boosted to 12 or 14 to 1. Stripped down and with a higher compression, *Autocar* confirmed, the Hotshot did 84 mph.

Popular Science was particularly impressed with the Hotshot's performance, appearance, construction and "dual personality" of roadster and racer. The magazine ran a four-page feature on the Hotshot, showing the bare frame, the car stripped down and running on a track, and more.

"America's own sport car?" The Hotshot may have been exactly that. At least it was the first sports car in regular production here. Before the Corvette, the Cunningham or the Thunderbird, the Hotshot was ready to get down and dirty on the race track. The illustration shows how the Hotshot can be quickly changed from a closed to an open-top sports car, or even stripped down for racing with every bit of useless weight and drag-inducing paraphernalia removed. *Banks Collection*

Powel Crosley's target price for the Hotshot was $849, less than that of any other Crosley. But as usual the announced price was optimistic. Two weeks after it was introduced the Hotshot was advertised by dealers for $935 to $995, delivered. At least Crosley could still say it cost under a thousand.

Once again, Crosley was going after the common man, the same market he had targeted with his low-cost radios in 1921, and again in 1939 with the first Crosley automobile. In a lengthy letter to dealers that introduced the Hotshot, he was also reaching out to the sport-minded, those for whom an exciting little roadster would be an attractive toy, be they rich or poor. And for anyone who wanted transportation for just one or two people, Crosley maintained, the Hotshot would fill the bill nicely. For them, sportiness would be a bonus. Not a necessity, but a nice touch.

The miniscule sports car's design was a complete departure from anything Crosley Motors had attempted. The engine was just about the only thing it had in common with other Crosleys. But Powel Crosley was written all over it, in bits and pieces that saved money and made the car stand out: no grille, for example (the air intake was beneath the bumper), and the lockable engine-access plate in the middle of the hood. Both saved money in production, and the dinner tray-size hatch eliminated hinges, springs and a latch mechanism. Both also made people look.

As this factory photo illustrates, the Hotshot could be stripped down for racing in minutes. Removing the top and supports, the spare tire and its mounting hardware, the bumpers, headlights, running lights and windshield took off over 100 pounds of excess weight—and it reduced wind drag. No special tools required! Crosley publicity called the Hotshot "the car with a dual personality." *Banks Collection*

DOWN-TO-EARTH FLYING—that's the feeling you get when you let out the road-hugging Crosley Hotshot. The Hotshot has combined leaf and coil spring rear suspension, and strut-type hydraulic shock absorbers all round to give the smooth, shock-free road hugging ability necessary in racing type vehicles. Easily detachable side doors and attractive all-weather tailored top and side curtains (not shown) are standard equipment. Equipped for Crosley heater and radio.

WEEK-END FOR TWO and it's a wonderful week-end the moment you slip behind the wheel of the Crosley Hotshot. Plenty of space to stow away luggage for a few days or a long trip. The Hotshot makes going places fun—so smooth, so easy to handle. Gets admiring attention everywhere.

WORLD'S RECORD MADE BY CROSLEY POWERED SPEED-BOAT! A Crosley powered hydroplane, piloted by Jack Van Deman, of Philadelphia, recently established a new world's record of 52.250 miles per hour. The 44 cu. in. speedster cracked all records in establishing this 48 cu. in. record.

One wonders who was responsible for the styling? Could Powel Crosley have designed this car on his own? The curves, the fenders, the rear deck—all the elements that are so important to the overall *style* of an automobile—who designed those? What inspired it?

As Crosley said in a letter to dealers introducing the Hotshot, he had been a fan of roadsters since he saw his first Ford roadster in 1904, but the Hotshot was worlds beyond the Ford Model N. Powel Crosley liked to say that the Hotshot was inspired by the classic race cars of Europe—like the one in his garage. Crosley owned a 1948 Jaguar XK-120, one of the first in the United States.

Taking a long look at the XK-120, it is possible to see elements that it shared with the Hotshot. There are

The brochure's final page shows that the Hotshot is a fun and friendly car, too. It's casual, and small enough to drive around the yard and pool. It's a great car for a couple who want to get away for a weekend, with the promise of all the room you need to carry holiday supplies. And of course the car is zippy—thanks to its CIBA engine, which has set world records powering hydroplanes. *Banks Collection*

To get at the CIBA engine powering the Hotshot, you had to unlock and lift off an access hatch. With access from underneath the car as well as through the top just about any repair or maintenance job could be accomplished. *Photo by Bill Angert*

The rear of a Hotshot has an exotic mixture of curves, blending into the pebble shield. This one of course has the optional spare tire in place (the tire mount came with it from the factory, but the wheel and tire cost extra). *Photo by Michael Banks*

Slightly bulbous when viewed head-on, the Hotshot looked like no other car. It kept the same body style from its introduction in 1948 through the end in 1952. *Photo courtesy of Karl Schultz*

the long front end and short rear deck, the high hood, headlamps mounted inboard of the fenders and the protruding grille area. The swoop to the passenger cabin from front and rear is more pronounced, but it's the same general idea used in the Jaguar. All of which is not to say that the Hotshot was anywhere near as beautiful as the Jaguar XK-120; but the British sports car must certainly have been a point of inspiration.

One element of the Hotshot's design was completed before Powel Crosley ever conceived of the car: the fenders. The Hotshot's fender shapes were taken directly from an earlier Crosley: the CC "roundsides" model pickup truck. No doubt in a hurry to get the Hotshot into production, Powel Crosley authorized using side-stampings for CC pickup front ends (fenders) to build Hotshot bodies, an idea that was credited to Lewis Crosley. A glance at a 1947 pickup and the Hotshot shows the similarities. The Hotshot's front wheel well was given a squared-off look at the top with a piece of steel that

A view of a Hotshot's interior. The leather above the dashboard is not standard. Standard Hotshot cockpits had rubber cockpit trim. It appears that Crosley Motors found yet another way to save money by using leftover CC gauges on the dashboard. Deciding to save money by reusing the old gauges (or new ones of the same design) may be the cause of Crosley turning down whatever Tjaarda designed. The radio in this unit is the standard option, but the speaker grille is either a new design made for the Hotshot, or owner-made. The top is the standard black with red trim. *Photo by Jim Bollman*

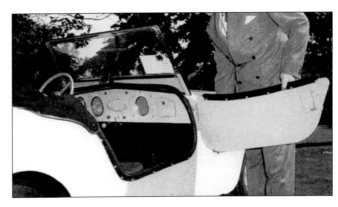

Mounting an optional Hotshot half-door was a simple matter of fitting two pins into two slots. *Banks Collection*

was added in. Later, the old CC stamping templates were modified to include these.

The design saved money, and, as Paul Gorrell points out, made Crosley perhaps the only automaker to use old truck fenders on new sports cars. Of course, those were the same fenders used on all Crosleys. (Those keeping track of Crosley cost-reducing methods can add this to the similarity between the design of the Hotshot's windshield and those of prewar Crosleys. There is also the fact that the Hotshot offered only a fabric roof—more savings in steel.)

Assume the Hotshot's general lines—the high hood, prominent radiator shell, and other elements mentioned three paragraphs back—were inspired by the Jaguar XK-120. Add that to the fact that Hotshot fenders were literally taken from a three year-old vehicle, and you have a car designed in part by Powel Crosley, Lewis Crosley and, if you credit him for the fender shape due to his participation in the design of the CC's slab-sided fenders, Carl Sundberg.

But those elements left the design nowhere near complete. What would go between those fenders? The cockpit, engine and chassis. Details of the hood and rear deck, the cockpit entry and doors—and other elements. It is unlikely that Lewis or Powel Crosley had the design experience necessary to create the entire car (possible, but not likely). Not when they had routinely

hired designers for decades to create the forms and styles of radios, refrigerators, home appliances, furniture and other consumer products in a highly competitive market. And they had used professional designers to help them with automobile designs in the past.

The angles and curves of the Hotshot's front and rear deck were more complex than the fenders. The same was true of the slope and curves of the hood. These elements and the interior would have needed a professional's touch.

We do know that Crosley Motors hired famed designer John Tjaarda to do a treatment for the Hotshot's dashboard. Tjaarda charged $5,000 and Powel Crosley rejected the design. Stories vary as to whether Carl Sundberg, who specialized in industrial design, helped with the Hotshot's design. It is true that Sundberg worked on the initial postwar Crosley design, and he had extensive experience in auto body design with General Motors before starting his own firm with Montgomery Ferar in 1934. But thus far those elements of Sundberg's career, and his earlier connection with Crosley via the 1939 New York World's Fair are the only evidence that he was a likely candidate to have worked on the Hotshot.

An equally likely candidate is Count Alexis de Sakhnoffsky. Sakhnoffsky's specialty was automobile design. As a young man he worked for Vanden Plas coachworks in Belgium, and designed a number of custom sports car bodies. In America in the 1930s, he did endless work for Lebaron, Murray and other body companies, and was responsible for the Auburn boat-tailed speedster. And he did quite a bit of work on the design of the American Austin, and later the American Bantam—at reduced rates. Sakhnoffsky worked on even smaller cars in the form of a series of award-winning juvenile pedal cars for Murray. Jokes about the pedal cars aside, he certainly had solid experience in small cars.

In addition to his qualifications, Sakhnoffsky had one definite connection with the Hotshot. He did an exquisite series of sketches of the cars that were used in advertising and in the Hotshot brochure shown in this chapter. He also illustrated the 1950 Crosley full-line brochure. Oddly, Crosley credited his artwork in the brochures. (Sakhnoffsky and Paul Klotsch were the only people Powel Crosley ever credited.)

While the Hotshot created excitement in the press, among racers and at Crosley Motors, it had a short first model year and sold only 752 units. Unhappily, the rest of the Crosley lineup did not do well, either. Crosley's best-selling model was the station wagon, and only 3,803 of those came off the line—a dead drop of 84 percent from 1948's total. Wrapping up the list were 2,231 sedans, 645 convertibles and 287 trucks.

A total production of only 7,718 cars and trucks in 1949 left Crosley Motors trailing even Nash and Kaiser, though ahead of Hudson and Willys Jeepster. On October 12, Crosley announced a net loss of $1,030,309 for the 1949 fiscal year ending July 31. The preceding year (when all those wagons were sold) the company had a net profit of $1,496,874. Sales had fallen by half from the previous year.

For what it might be worth, Powel Crosley, Jr., seemed to have the small-car market pretty much to himself. Such postwar small-car upstarts as the Bobbi Car, the three-wheel Davis, the Keller and the Playboy were gone or were fading fast. And Ford, General Motors and Chrysler were finished with small cars—at least for the moment.

Being the only player on the field didn't guarantee success. All auto manufacturers had seen sales slow down. One after another—starting with Ford in February—automakers began lowering their prices to stimulate sales. Crosley waited and watched as Packard, Willys, General Motors, Kaiser-Frazer and others fell into line.

Powel Crosley, Jr., didn't feel he could join the trend. There was less room in Crosley's pricing structure to

A rare color banner for the Hotshot: "America's Own Sport Car!" *Banks Collection*

absorb cuts. But sales continued to drop throughout the summer and into the fall, and Crosley management knew something had to be done. In October Crosley Motors finally cut prices on all models. The cuts ranged from $51 to $105. The price of the station wagon, for example, dropped from $999 to $894. The Sedan DeLuxe and the Club Convertible each would cost $866, a reduction of $101. The Hotshot was cut from $912 to $861.

Crosley Motors could ill-afford the cuts, even though some of the cost was borne by dealers. Speaking at a level of obfuscation that he reserved for subjects that disturbed him, Powel Crosley announced that reductions were made as a result of "cost-reducing research and development," as though his engineers had made some sort of scientific breakthrough. This "research and development" likely was focused on ways to cut waste, find cheaper suppliers and recycle left-over material. No doubt a hard eye was cast on the efficiency of the men on the assembly line, too.

Also in October 1949, the 1950 Hotshot was announced. The full 1950 line was formally introduced in mid-December in New York. Crosley said that the company had completed its tooling for the 1950 models with no increases in pricing. The main reason there were no increases in pricing was because there were no real changes in the cars for 1950.

CHAPTER 7
1950: Competition and Additions

Ford and Chevrolet coasted through 1950 on their 1949 styling, with only a few minor changes in chrome and other elements. Chrysler did the same. Powel Crosley and his crew most likely breathed a sigh of relief when they saw the 1950 designs, for no changes were forthcoming in Crosley's styling. There was no money for it, and Crosley Motors had no choice but to continue with what it had, against cars that were selling in the hundreds of thousands.

The 1949 and 1950 models were so much alike that it appears that some of the photos of 1950 models sent to newspapers and magazines may have been shots of 1949 models. In advertising, images used in 1949 ads were recycled in 1950 ads, sometimes mirrored, sometimes not. Brochure art was also recycled.

The 1950 Crosleys were announced in New York on January 24, 1950. Each of the four passenger cars and two trucks were priced under $1,000, a major marketing advantage to Powel Crosley's way of thinking. All models still sported disc brakes, front and rear turn signals, and undercoating as standard equipment. Prices (including delivery to New York) were:

    Station wagon: $959
    Club convertible: $929
    Deluxe sedan: $929
    Panel truck (sedan delivery): $909
    Hotshot: $899
    Pickup truck: $884

A Crosley factory price list from March 1950 shows higher prices for the same vehicles. Delivery is not included:

    Station wagon: $999
    Club convertible: $967
    Deluxe sedan: $967
    Panel truck (sedan delivery): $939
    Hotshot: $935
    Pickup truck: $908

These prices ranged from $500 to $900 less than the closest competing vehicles, and they were higher than 1949 model prices. (Price cuts were announced almost immediately.) Of course, Crosleys couldn't match the

A "1950" Crosley station wagon that is actually a 1949 model. This photo was used on the cover of the 1950 Crosley Motors brochure, but first appeared on the cover of the 1949 brochure. The hood sports the ornament originally added near the end of the 1948 model year, and placed on all 1949 and 1950 models. This car of course has sliding glass windows, but roll-down windows were added to the Crosley line in mid-1950.

competition in size or performance but, as Powel Crosley liked to say, "You can't build a big car for a small amount of money." It followed that you couldn't buy a big car for small money, either.

Or could you? It was now possible to buy an 8-year-old used car for half the cost of a new Crosley. (In 1949 Powel Crosley was bragging that a new Crosley could be had for the same price as an 8-year-old used car.) A newer used car, like a 1948 Studebaker Champion, could be had for $1,395—$400 more than a Crosley sedan. By the end of 1949, a buyer might find a 1949 Plymouth Club Coupe for $1,095, and even a 1949 Ford two-door for less than $1,100. There was the odd bargain, too—like a 1946 Willys station wagon for $895. Each of these examples included a radio and heater, extra-cost options on a Crosley.

With the price gap beginning to close, Powel Crosley continued to push the car's economy, its small size and safety. But gasoline averaged 23 cents per gallon and was no longer rationed. True, the big cars were getting only 15 to 20 miles per gallon, but saving a penny or so per mile meant little now. Plus, the new cars looked grand and had standard features Crosleys lacked. Compared with most of the Crosleys, they had lots of power—even the six-cylinder models.

And the new Dodges, Chevys, Studebakers and other American cars had lots of room. This was important to thousands of recently-married couples of the postwar era. Families would be growing from two to four or six as children came along. And the children themselves would grow, all too soon to the point where trying to pack three or four into the tiny back seat of a Crosley wagon or sedan was asking for noisy, unhappy kids.

Still, Powel Crosley pushed the idea of owning a small car for its own sake. A small car was easier to park, he maintained, and could make its way through heavy traffic with ease. Another advantage of a small car was safety. Overall, conventional wisdom had it that you were safer in a large car, but in 1948 Crosley told an interviewer for *Kiplinger's Personal Finance* magazine that a Crosley "comes out creditably in collisions with heavier vehicles." The magazine reported that Crosley carried with him "…a folder with photographs of collisions between Crosleys and an assortment of Buicks, Chryslers and Fords, to illustrate this point." His idea was that a Crosley would "bounce off" a larger car because of its light weight, rather than stay in place and sustain damage.

Even backed up by the photos (which, after all, could be cherry-picked) the statement was a little difficult to believe. Crosley's argument that the Crosley's small size gave it maneuverability necessary to get out of a dangerous situation fast was hard to take, too. People involved in accidents usually don't see them coming. Nor was it likely that the motoring public accepted Crosley's assurances that drivers of larger cars would automatically be more careful around a small Crosley.

But there still were people who appreciated saving a penny a mile, and some who believed Crosley's safety points. And there were some who simply *liked* the Crosley, just as some folks liked Packards or Hudsons—then and now.

As always, Powel Crosley was coming up with new ideas. He seems to have started tinkering with the Hotshot not long after it was introduced. Early in 1950 along came the Super Sports, an upscale version of the Hotshot that was rolled out at the 1950 Sportsman's Show at New York's Grand Central Palace, on February 17. The Super Sports on display was a special model with imported South American leopard fur seat and floor

This is the special hood ornament that adorned all of the Crosley "Super" models, including the Super Sports. *Photo by Michael Banks*

covering. The regular Super Sports (without leopard covering) was priced at $950.

Crosley's first brochure for 1950 tentatively mentioned the car, but gave few details. In a small paragraph under the heading, "The Dashing Crosley Hotshot," it noted that the Hotshot "…is also made under the name Super Sports; incorporating folding top, zipper side curtains, complete plastic leather cockpit edge trim and liner matching the red upholstery, at slightly higher price." Some thought of it as a "Super Hotshot."

The Super Sports was introduced again in June, along with an entire Crosley "Super" line. This time the brochure was up-front about the Super Sports. It described the car as having a "folding top, zipper side curtains, complete plastic leather cockpit edge trim and liner, matching the red upholstery—PLUS all the features of its companion sports roadster, the Hotshot." A special "bird" hood ornament was designed for the car, and the Super Sports featured a "Super" emblem in place of the Hotshot emblem just ahead of the cockpit on each side. The folding top was more expansive than that of the Hotshot, and easier to rig.

The Super Sports engine was the same as those of other Crosleys—for now. Some factory tuning had taken the compression ratio from 7.8:1 to 8:1.

The Hotshot and Super Sports both developed an enthusiastic following among sports-car buffs and racers. But sales were not outstanding in 1950; together the roadsters sold a total of 742.

While the 1950 Crosleys seemed to be the same as the 1949s, that would change with the Super line.

Compared with the Hotshot, the Super Sports had a roomier top that was easier to put up and take down. *Photos by Bill Angert*

While not based on a completely new design, the Supers would be an upgrade for the entire Crosley line. As with past mid-year changes, Powel Crosley hoped the Super models would breathe new life into Crosley Motors. All Supers, except the Hotshot/Super Sports, had roll-up windows—a major change no doubt welcomed by buyers. The Supers also featured the bird hood ornament that the Super Sports wore, and a fender ornament on each side. They came with shock absorbers on all four wheels, a line of chrome trim running along the front fenders and doors, and cloth upholstery.

Standard Crosley passenger vehicles and trucks were promoted to "Deluxe" status, carrying the same hood ornaments that previously marked Crosley Deluxe vehicles. The new Deluxe models had no chrome trims and old-style upholstery, but they did have roll-up windows.

The Super models may have been Powel Crosley's response to poor sales during the first part of the model year. At this point, he probably had to pour more cash into the ailing company. But it wasn't finished; Crosley still a few more cards left to play.

While it seemed that small cars were on the way out, at least one was in the works as far back as 1948. George W. Mason, Chairman of Nash-Kelvinator, had a buddy named Lewis Crosley—the same Lewis Crosley whose brother was President and Treasurer of Crosley Motors. The two frequently played golf at Biscayne Bay, Florida. Mason had been a friendly competitor of Crosley Radio and the Crosley Corporation when he was Chairman and CEO of the Kelvinator Corporation during the 1920s and '30s. Crosley and Kelvinator

Inside, the Super Sports offered the same prewar gauge set as the Hotshot. *Photo by Bill Angert*

A Super Sports chassis. *Photo courtesy of Karl Schultz*

were two of the largest refrigerator manufacturers in the world. When Kelvinator became Nash-Kelvinator (just as Powel Crosley was beginning work on his car), Mason found himself in the automobile business, as well. Thus, he paid a lot of attention to Crosley enterprises. He received regular updates as to the progress of Crosley Motors, and watched the company and its products with more than a little interest and admiration.

Mason thought that Crosley had the right idea, but the wrong approach. A small, economical car, he decided, could be a good seller, if it was not associated in the consumer mind with low budgets, tight quarters and little comfort. It was easy to see that Powel Crosley was fixated on the attention-getting value of an ultra-small car, and convinced that there were tens of thousands of people out there who couldn't afford or wouldn't pay a few hundred dollars more for a roomier, more comfortable and better-appointed car—one that still saved on gas, but which had a bit more power and accommodated the driver and passengers better. Mason felt otherwise, and he could see that the Crosley was not going to get any bigger, nor was it going to leave the ultra-low-cost route it had traveled since its beginnings.

Mason was fascinated with small cars, even though he was a physically huge man. He was also interested in high-tech, most of all aerodynamics. Under his guidance, Nash became one of the first automakers to experiment with wind tunnels, which resulted in the aerodynamic Nash Airflyte models of 1949. Concurrent with this, Mason investigated small-car designs, and reached the conclusion that "small" did not have to mean "stripped-down" as it did with the Crosley.

Intended to compete in the low-price market the Nash Rambler's size was calculated to make it more efficient to build and save its owners money in operating costs. Nash made the car a convertible, perhaps following Crosley's lead from the prewar models. (The Rambler also used the same cant rail system to support the top as Crosley did.) This not only saved operating costs by lowering weight, but also saved resources. Using less material was important, with the Korean War and the prospect of limitations on the availability of critical materials like steel.

The final design, presented to the public in April 1950, was larger than the Crosley, with a 100-inch wheelbase compared to Crosley's 80, and an overall length of 176 inches, versus Crosley at 145 inches. The Rambler's width was 73-1/2 inches, while the Crosley sedan was 49 inches wide. The Rambler easily seated five people.

At 2,500 pounds, the Rambler was over twice the weight of the Crosley sedan. It used a larger engine—a six-cylinder of 83 horsepower—but still got 30 miles per gallon.

The Rambler's aerodynamic shape followed those of other new Nash products. It was attractive in its time, although it appears short and squat today. It was a foot shorter than its main competitors, low-end models from Chevrolet, Ford and Plymouth. But it felt plenty large to drivers, and most were satisfied with its power.

The Rambler sold 9,330 its first year, along with nearly 3,000 two-door station wagons. Priced at $1,873, the Rambler convertible included the Nash "conditioned air heater," a clock, a modern one-piece windshield, turn signals, wheel covers, and superior upholstery—and two windshield wipers.

In its second year, Rambler would offer two-door station wagons and hardtop coupes. Over 34,000 1951 all-steel wagons would be sold, plus 15,000 convertibles and 19,000 hardtop coupes. The line would carry the company all the way to its AMC days, and provide plenty of proof that small cars, done properly, could succeed. It almost certainly took some sales from Crosley.

While George Mason was enjoying the sudden success of the Rambler, Powel Crosley was putting more money into Crosley Motors while he dealt with a new technological problem. The Crosley's disc brakes turned out to have a very specific problem. The brakes tended to lock up when traveling roads in northern states that were salted in the winter. Midway through 1950, Crosley production shifted to 9-inch Bendix hydraulic shoe brakes, and stayed with them. (Goodyear/Hawley sued Crosley Motors over ordering over 9,000 of sets of brakes, and then neither accepting nor paying for them. The case was settled out of court.)

The pressure of being Powel Crosley, Jr., must have been intense by this time, with Crosley Motors waiting to see the reaction to its Super models, and hoping that the disc brake debacle would not have negative fallout. And suddenly there was serious competition in the small-car field. The Nash Rambler was getting rave reviews. And scheduled to begin production in June 1950 was another new small car, the Henry J, built for the person of average means. Or, as Henry J. Kaiser, the man behind the car and its name, put it, a car "… with a price that will be within the budgets of millions who have never been able to afford the purchase of a new automobile."

It sounded a lot like Powel Crosley talking about his car. The new car, from Kaiser-Frazer, would get 30 to 35 miles per gallon, and would be built without the costly and ornamental "frills" that were built into most automobiles. It was designed to be built with the fewest possible components. Like Crosleys, it did not have a trunk lid, to save on stamping costs. The rear windows were fixed, and armrests, glove box, air vents and passenger-side sun visor were eliminated.

The Henry J was not a big hit, in part because its $1,300 price tag was not that much lower than competing models from the Big 3, and because it was essentially a stripped-down car. Sales were reported in the tens of thousands the first year, but quickly fell off until 1954, when production was around 1,000 and the car was suspended. Branded as the "Allstate" and sold through Sears, it had very poor sales. So did a Japanese version. Like the Rambler, the Henry J had probably taken some sales from Crosley. But Crosley was in trouble before either car was even announced.

Just as this new competition entered the market, Crosley was preoccupied with expanding the Crosley Motors lineup with a completely new vehicle called the "Farm-O-Road."

The Crosley Farm-O-Road was designed to be used as a farm vehicle (often in place of a tractor) as well as a passenger vehicle. At a July 19 showing in New York, the initial delivered price was announced as $895. The factory price was soon set at $795. Newspaper stories described the Farm-O-Road as having add-on farm implements that could be raised by hydraulic lift to convert it to a roadable vehicle. (Smart owners would be removing the tools before hitting the road.)

The CIBA engine powered the Farm-O-Road (FOR) and its optional front and rear power-takeoff units for implements. The FOR had a heavy-duty rear axle and conventional and auxiliary transmissions, with six forward speeds and two reverse.

In its standard form, the FOR had a two-passenger main body with a small cargo area at the rear. A dump-bed could be attached to carry passengers or just about any kind of payload. The front end reminded some people of the military Jeep, with its high, square hood and wide, flat fenders. It had a 63-inch wheelbase and 40-inch tread, which meant it could drive a lot of roads and trails that other vehicles couldn't.

Options included the aforementioned power takeoffs and dump bed, as well as a rear seat for the dump bed, the passenger-side windshield wiper, 4:1 gear trans-

The original Crosley Farm-O-Road. This sturdy little vehicle was built to serve at an endless number of tasks. It could be driven on normal roads, or off-road. Dual rear wheels, optional power take-offs, and a surprising number of add-on tools turned the Farm-O-Road into a do-everything machine. In addition to being a good idea, it was solid vehicle with an attractive appearance. The unit shown here is an original 1949 prototype. *Photo by Bill Angert*

A rear view shows the Farm-O-Road's standard cargo area, in which people might ride—hang on! The front seat cushions were appropriately thick. *Photo by Bill Angert*

The gauge setup on the dashboard was simple, and appears to use the same CC-style gauges used with the Super Sports. Note the 70-mph top speed. *Photo by Bill Angert*

A peek at the Farm-O-Road's engine compartment. *Photo by Bill Angert*

This view shows the (probably optional) spare tire and the vehicle's standard emblem. *Photo by Bill Angert*

fer and dual rear wheels. An optional fabric top/cover formed a body with zippered side doors and a rear flap. Tool and implement options included:

- Bar mower
- Post-hole digger
- Snow blade
- Front-mount 3-blade chopper mower
- Disk harrow
- Hay rake
- Gang reel mower (3)
- Cultivator
- 10-inch plow
- Sickle mower
- Skis for front wheels

After one or two 1949 prototypes, the Farm-O-Road was manufactured from 1950 through 1952. It was never changed. All serial numbers begin with "FR." It is estimated that fewer than 600 FORs were built. Powel Crosley's motto for the FOR was, "Twice the work of a work horse. Twice the speed of a race horse."

With the Korean War looming, Crosley Motors once again looked toward possible government funding. This time the concept was a "personnel carrier," presumably for use to transport people and small loads around a military base. As it had done during the previous war, the company stripped-down a version of one of its standard vehicles: the station wagon. The top and sides above the belt line were removed (or omitted). There were no doors, only kickpans welded in place level with the seat bottoms. The tailgate was left out. The cargo compartment was taken up by two side-facing bench seats, which could accommodate four people (six, if they weren't too large). The normal driver and passenger seats up front provided seating for two more.

Even with the introduction of the Supers and the Farm-O-Road, 1950 was a downhill year for Crosley Motors. Only 7,197 Crosley vehicles were sold, with the station wagon responsible for more than half the year's business.

Glimpses of new designs were coming out of Detroit. The 1951 Fords in particular had some distinctly different styling touches and lower prices. The Chevrolet was spruced up, and even Chrysler's products were looking fresh, though pricing was high. With new competition from Nash and others, Crosley would have to do some restyling to stay in the game.

Powel Crosley's new "Army car" was a personnel transport based on a 1950 Crosley station wagon. Like his World War II concept, the car was stripped of doors and rear body, and equipped with seating accommodations. As can be seen in this photo, the transport carried a spare tire in the standard position used by all Crosley vehicles. *Banks Collection*

Another look at Crosley's Military personnel transport. It was tested at Eglin Air Force Base in Florida, but not accepted. *Banks Collection*

A Crosley personnel transport done up in U.S. Army colors, with a standard olive drab paint job. *Photo courtesy of Jim Bollman*

CHAPTER 8
1951-1952: The End

To kick off the introduction of the 1951 Crosleys, Powel Crosley spent $20,000-plus for a full-page ad in *The Saturday Evening Post*'s December 1950 issue. This ad called up the specter of gas rationing with the line, *"Crosley still gives you 35 to 50 miles on a gallon of regular gasoline—and didn't you wish you had a car that could do that the last time gasoline was rationed?"*

Gasoline wasn't being rationed, but the possibility of America getting involved in another protracted overseas war made rationing a possibility. It was a time of rumors of mobilization and commodities regulation. Speculation also swirled about the suspension of automaking and home building. None of these things happened immediately, but they were foremost in the minds of everyone. The Crosley Motors ad played on the worries of most Americans.

The advertisement was more effective in simply reminding the public that the 1951 Crosleys existed. The line now consisted of nine models, including the Super Sports, the new Farm-O-Road and a business coupe which was essentially a sedan with no back seat and sliding windows on the door. Adding Super passenger cars to the mix gave Crosley a total of 11 models. (If there were any Super pickups or panel trucks, they were special orders or modified by dealers or owners.)

By the time the ad appeared in *The Saturday Evening Post*, the Crosley Supers and the Farm-O-Road had been on the scene for six months, so there was little new about Crosleys. However, at the very end of 1950 an event brought Crosley Motors more favorable attention than any advertisement could have done.

The event was the first running of the Sam Collier Memorial Grand Prix at Sebring, Florida, on December 31. Destined to become one of the most important events in sports car racing, it was sponsored by the Sports Car Club of America (SCCA). It was a "formula" race, which meant that entries competed based on a formula that equalized the difference in performance of cars of varying engine displacements. A car with a large engine, for example, might have to run a longer distance than a car with a smaller engine.

The first Sebring race lasted six hours, and involved a

This expensive, full-page ad appeared in the December 1950 issue of *The Saturday Evening Post*, a hopeful attempt to place fuel economy in the public consciousness. In the ad, Crosley used the potential for war in Korea to highlight the Crosley's fuel economy. *Banks Collection*

twisting three-and-a-half mile course laid out around a former Army Air Force base (Hendricks Field). It is today a 12-hour race that is ranked with the 24 Hours of Daytona and the 24 Hours of Le Mans races in prestige. Sebring draws some of the world's best-known drivers and sports car manufacturers.

A Crosley Hostshot was entered in the 1950 race almost by accident. Vic Sharpe, who owned the local Crosley franchise, happened to drive a Hotshot to the track to deliver tires to a friend who had entered a

116

Cadillac-powered Allard. A friend suggested that the Hotshot might have a chance at winning the race under the handicapping system. Fred (Frits) Koster and Ralph Deshon drove the car, as Sharpe was not licensed to compete by the SCCA.

The Hotshot won the race, and the first Sam Collier trophy. Crosley made much of the win in advertising, especially since far more expensive and powerful cars like the Allard and Ferraris were run against it. It would not be the last time a Hotshot made sports-car racing history. In 1951 a Hotshot placed second in the Tokyo Grand Prix, and won the Swiss Grand Prix (*Grand de la Suisse*). From there the Hotshot went on to dominate many courses. Other makes of cars powered by the CIBA also racked up a significant number of wins and places during the 1950s. Among them the Bandini, Devin Hotshot, Ermini, Fiat, Fibersport, Moretti, Nardi, and Siata.

A Hotshot also competed in the 1951 Le Mans Grand Prix in France. It was specially modified for the race. The engine was rebuilt and tuned at the Crosley factory. An aluminum crankcase and steel crankshaft were added, plus a special cam and other improvements. Horsepower was increased to 42. The body was a custom build made in Indianapolis by race-car builder Floyd Dryer.

After only two hours at the race in France, the generator began to seize up. The Hotshot was out of the race before it was properly started, even though it was moving up in its formula class and was taking laps on the track at 73 miles per hour. The little car was capable of 100 miles per hour and most people who saw the race agreed that it would have won, had it not suffered the generator problem. The Hotshot was repaired and went on to win at Watkins Glen and elsewhere.

The problem with restyling automobile bodies was that, while the practice at least got attention and hopefully generated sales, it cost a lot of money. But it had been a necessary element in automaking since Alfred Sloane of General Motors introduced the concept of "planned obsolescence." Automobile designs typically changed in an evolutionary fashion from year to year, as it was a firm belief among most automakers that radical changes would be rejected by the public. Every now and then something really new got through, as with the Nash Airflyte and Rambler models, the 1949 Ford and the Crosley CCs and CDs. But for the most part successful automobile designs grew from previous successes.

So it was that the 1951 Ford, Chevrolet and Chrysler products were styled without major changes in profiles

A Crosley flyer celebrating a Hotshot's win at the 1950 Sam Collier Memorial Trophy Race at Sebring. This was the first Sebring Grand Prix and the Hotshot was entered almost by accident. The car's number, 19, was hastily applied with black shoe polish. *Banks Collection*

George Schraft and Phil Stiles entered this modified Hotshot in the 1951 Le Mans Grand Prix. The engine was modified at the Crosley factory, and the body built in Indianapolis. Had it not been for a faulty generator, the Crosley Hotshot would have won the 1951 Le Mans. *Banks Collection*

or general appearance. But a lot of details were changed, details that added up to a new look. This was most evident in the 1949 Ford.

Both Ford and Chevrolet retained their general body lines, but made dramatic changes to their front ends. Ford dropped the bullet-nose look by eliminating the large cone and nacelle centered in its grille. In its place were two bullets in smaller nacelles, set in a single grille bar with a de-emphasized line of chrome above it. The bumper, grille crossbar and its framing curve of chrome combined with the Ford badge and hood ornament made a pyramid-like pattern. Other 1951 changes included emphasizing the chrome on the fenders and doors, and extending the taillight housings from the rear halfway to the C-pillars on each side, like small wings. Some Fords, like the Victoria Custom hardtop coupe, had reversed C-pillars with wrap-around rear windows.

Chevrolet also went with a pyramid structure, the base of which was marked with the wide bumper—above was a crosspiece with running lights and turn signals at each side. The middle was a squared, inward-turned arch, with the whole thing topped off by the Chevrolet emblem beneath a crowning hood ornament. The rear fenders almost puffed out from the body, and the rear deck rose above them, just as the hood rose over the front fenders.

The Plymouth's grille seemed to echo the Chevrolet's in an understated way. Otherwise, the car carried over its conservative lines from 1950.

Just as it had in 1950, Crosley Motors followed a path similar to that of the Big 3. The basic body style—the same as 1949's—was retained, but the car underwent a lot of detail work. Up front, the grille was reduced to two wings—each larger than the previous model's. In the center of the upper wing was a nacelle. It had no cone, but even the most casual glance reminded the viewer strongly of the 1940 and '50 Fords.

There were other differences between the Crosley's styling and that of its competition. The tops of the Crosley's fenders were flatter than Ford's and its hood rose higher

The cover of the 1951 Crosley brochure carried the motto, "America's Most Needed Car!" The emphasis was on the most-changed element: the grille. The artwork depicts a Crosley Super convertible as seen from straight-on. *Banks Collection*

The Crosley station wagon was the best-selling model for 1951. A total of 4,500 wagons—Deluxe and Super—would be sold. The Deluxe (formerly standard) wagon had the old sliding windows; the Super had roll-down windows. The back seat of the standard wagon could be removed, while the Super's removable seat could also be folded up out of the way. *Banks Collection*

The 1951 Crosley's grille was composed of two wing-like cross-pieces with a nacelle—like that of an aircraft engine—in the center. This prominent addition to an otherwise pedestrian front end reminded many people of the 1949 and 1950 Ford grilles. *Photo by Michael Banks*

at a steeper angle. But what was previously the most dramatic element of the Ford was now the most dramatic element of the Crosley: the "bullet nose." Over half a century later, car people still wonder if Crosley "swiped" the bullet nose from Ford, and casual observers have been known to ask whether a given 1951 or 1952 Crosley *is* a Ford.

Again, Ford had moved on to the two-nacelle look for 1951. So there was probably no grumbling at Ford about whether Crosley was infringing on Ford's design. And the Crosley did look good. Had Crosley put a cone in its nacelle, it may have been too much like Ford. So there was no cone—but there was an optional addition for the nacelle: a propeller. It complemented the aviation elements of wings and "engine" nacelle perfectly, and gave the Crosley the ultimate "airplane-like" touch. Nobody knows how many propellers the factory put on Crosleys, but probably almost as many were stolen or broken. Today, they are much sought-after by 1951 and 1952 Crosley owners. (Studebaker used the same thing in the design of its 1951 Commander. The prominent nose of the car had a nacelle that resembled a jet engine's intake, and a cone plus a propeller was mounted in it.)

Other style elements were largely left alone. As described previously, each Super model had a hood ornament, plus an ornament on each fender (something else Studebaker used). Supers also gained a chrome stripe from the front fender to the back of the door on each side. They were further set off by a "Super" logo on each side, just above the air vent. A beltline chrome strip ran from the end of the hood all the way back to the C-pillar. Inside, Supers had two sun visors, as opposed to the driver's-side-only visor that had been traditional. Super station wagons featured rear bench seats that could be folded up against the front seats, or removed, to increase the cargo area.

Other changes to the 1951 Crosley in general were an improved clutch, better seat padding, upgraded door and seat upholstery, and "full-fashioned" floor mats. The lights, bumpers, personality lines, door handles, windshield, rear windows and general body lines remained the same for all Crosleys, whether they were Deluxe (Standard) or Super.

As can be seen in this photo of a 1951 Crosley wagon, the external door hinges were kept in the new model. The personality lines on the front fenders are the same as in previous CDs, as are the external air vent and the split windshield. Wheels were usually painted off-white, rather than matching the body color as is the case here. All Supers featured chrome stripes on their front fenders and doors. The red interior was common for the Super. *Photo by Michael Banks*

Here can be seen the beltline chrome strip that separated the body from the top. This wagon is missing the part of the beltline strip that runs forward on the doors to the hood. The sliding glass windows were kept for the station wagon rear passengers, while the front windows on Supers were roll-up. (Sedans and business coupes had fixed rear windows.) This particular wagon has the side-opening rear door, as indicated by the door handle and lock at the right of the rear. The bumper guards, common to other Crosleys, had to be omitted because they would have blocked the door from opening. The passenger-side door has a lock, but the driver-side door does not. *Photo by Michael Banks*

This 1951 Super wagon has a complete beltline chrome strip, across the door and under the windshield plenum, stopping just where the hood begins. It also has a factory-option external mirror, but is missing the Super emblem. *Photo by Bill Angert*

The same wagon exhibits clamshell-style rear doors. The handle and lock are in one unit at the bottom center of the window. The lower door does not fold flat, but opens only to a 45-degree angle to accommodate the bumper guards. *Photo by Bill Angert*

The Super convertible sedan was described "as sports-like." As with the Super wagon and sedan, its rear seat could be folded up against the front seats. The rear window included a zipper, so airflow could be increased. *Photo by Bill Angert*

Comparing the rear of the 1949 sedan (inset) and the 1951 convertible shows there was no real difference between the styles (the top and the missing early emblem aside). While the front and sides had cosmetic changes, the rears were the same styling and stamping. The same was true of the top. The 1948 seems to be narrower, but that is because it has a higher profile with the top. *Banks Collection/Bill Angert*

The Super sedan was the jewel of Crosley Motors. Its rear seat was foldable, so it could be placed out of the way against the front seats. This offered more cargo area plus easier access to the trunk. *Banks Collection*

1951 dashboards saw no change, except for the appliqué covering on some. This may have originated with 1950 or earlier models. Note the parking brake handle, which had been a lever on the floor. The rubber covering on the gas, brake and clutch pedals was a fairly recent innovation for Crosleys. The windshield crank is, like many other parts of the car, smaller than average. The speedometer goes up to 70 where it once topped out at 60. *Photo by Bill Angert*

Here is a look into a Crosley trunk with the rear seat removed. This is the Super convertible in the preceding photos; you can make out the attachment points of the top, as well as part of one of the wood cant rails. The wheel wells can be seen at the bottom right and left. *Photo by Bill Angert*

As the Crosley Hotshot and Super Sports started to gain a reputation in sports car racing circles, the CIBA engine was catching on in hydroplane racing, too—enough that Crosley Motors' engine factory developed a special marine version of the CIBA. Manufacturers and individuals were building runabouts and racing boats powered by the 44-cubic-inch engine with no little success. In fact, the Crosley Marine Engine had set at least one world record. It offered a 9:1 compression ratio on regular gasoline. Business was so brisk that the company formed the Crosley Marine Engine Division.

Modifying Crosley engines became a minor industry for Nick Brajevich, better-known among Crosley owners as "Braj." After a part-time career of souping up cars of all sorts, Braje got involved in improving the Crosley CIBA for racers and those who simply wanted more speed. He eventually put together a business selling improved parts, carburetors and kits, called Braje Equipment. It is a sign of status among many Hotshot and Super Sports owners to have an engine with Braje parts.

Close-up of a Braje exhaust manifold and valve cover on a Crosley Super Sports. *Photo by Bill Angert*

The 1951 Crosley Hotshot was unchanged in looks. Both it and the Super Sports show no intake guards in the Crosley Motors brochures, so those may have been options. The Super Sports also retained its overall appearance, but had a new, unexpected feature: large, hinged doors that covered the entire opening. The side curtains that went with the top were designed to go over the inside and outside of the upper edge of the door, which made a big difference on cold days.

A Crosley Super Sports on display at the 1952 New York Auto Show. The model in her Irish golfer-themed costume seems prepared for a variety of sports. *Banks Collection*

The Super Sports continued to use the round CC-style instruments. The speedometer goes only to 70 miles per hour, but the car could do over 80. *Photo by Bill Angert*

This 1951 Super Sports was Powel Crosley's personal driver: note the "PC" license plate. A close look reveals that the car has contrasting black headlight pods (the body paint is red). The photo was taken behind his daughter, Page's, house on the Crosley estate, near a small artificial lake. *Banks Collection*

The big news for the Super Sports in 1951 was the addition of real doors on hinges, doors that covered the entire open areas next to the driver and passenger. This Super Sports has an optional outside mirror, and an optional radio with antenna. The covering of the dashboard (which matches the seats) continues down behind the door over the top edge of the passenger opening. *Photo by Bill Angert*

Another 1951 addition to the Crosley Super Sports was the "Quicksilver" engine option. (The name was invented by the same woman ad copywriter who dreamed up "Hydradisc" brakes.) It raised the CIBA engine's compression to 10:1, which increased horsepower and gave the Super Sports the highest compression of any stock American car. The option involved a device called the Thompson "Vitameter." It worked by adding a mixture of water, alcohol and tetraethyl lead to the air/fuel mixture, which eliminated wasted power and insured more compete combustion. The device was installed at the factory and only regular gasoline was required to achieve the 10:1 compression ratio.

While the Crosley line at large had so many changes, neither the pickup truck nor the panel truck (sedan delivery) had changed since 1949—except for the 1951 grille.

As sales continued to fall off, Crosley Motors lost dealers. Some were Nash dealers whose customers might have bought Crosleys but found Nash Ramblers more appealing economy cars. By July 1951 Macy's department store had dropped the Crosley, too. Gimbel's jumped in and took the franchise, eager to gain something from its rival. Prices hovered around $1,100:

- Super sedan: $1,095
- Super Sports: $1,097
- Super convertible: $1,095
- Super wagon: $1,133

All of the Deluxe Crosleys were over $1,000. The only Crosleys under $1,000 (just barely!) were the pickup truck ($995), the business coupe ($998) and maybe the basic Farm-O-Road. All Crosley prices were soon over $1,000. Powel Crosley blamed the high costs of labor and materials.

Powel Crosley's "small cars, small ads" philosophy had not changed. He would occasionally spring for a half- or full-page ad in a large magazine, but was still depending on small ads to bring in the business. Many ads continued to press the gas rationing theme. In the April 23, 1951, issue of *Life* magazine, one of Crosley's single-column ads led with rationing. "If gasoline rationing comes," read the headline, "do you have a car that will go 35 to 50 miles per gallon?" Recalling the hard times of World War II as the threat of a return to home-front conditions was raised by the Korean conflict, the ad promised, "150 miles of driving per week on an 'A' card while most other cars are getting only 30 to 40 miles."

Depending on your viewpoint, this could be considered slightly unethical, or simply clever marketing.

Here is a 1951 sedan delivery. As with the pickup truck it is plain except for the hood ornament, which it shared with Crosley Deluxe model passenger vehicles. The nacelle on the grille has no propeller. The two external mirrors were probably optional, but necessary in a vehicle with a limited rear view that might be blocked by cargo. *Banks Collection*

The Crosley pickup truck and panel truck were the same vehicles they had been for two years, except for the front-end treatment and the mechanical changes that were made to all Crosley vehicles. *Banks Collection*

Either way, invoking gas shortages didn't do much for Crosley Motors. This technique would be more effective in marketing the new Honda Civic twenty-odd years later. Perhaps Americans were more ready to accept rationing and shortages in 1951 than during 1973's oil crisis because in 1951 it was something in recent experience, something familiar that people knew they could survive.

Crosley's downward spiral continued. 1951 production totaled just 7,397 vehicles of all types. That was 200 more than 1950, but the company still took a loss. Crosley Motors advertising faded away, an indication of what was to come.

The 1952 Crosleys were exactly the same as 1951 models. Sales improved only slightly, and Crosley Motors was losing $500 per vehicle. Nothing the company did changed things, and Powel Crosley, Jr., was fresh out of ideas for products, production and marketing.

Employment was down to 1,054 from a high of 1,900. A majority of the workers probably were involved in building engines, because so few vehicles were built. Between January 1 and July 3, 1952, Crosley Motors turned out 2,466 cars and trucks.

In the face of ever-dwindling sales and mounting losses, Powel Crosley shut down Crosley Motors. Production ceased at the end of the day on Thursday, July 3, 1952.

1952's final accounting showed Crosley Motors as having sales of $5,617,542, with a net loss of $1,981,486. Engine and generator sales on the government contract were figured separately. The same had to be true for engines sold to companies using them to build their own vehicles, marine engines and engines sold to individuals, because the Crosley engine manufacturing operation was a very profitable enterprise. Had the engine plant's profits been included on the automotive balance sheets, the picture would have been very different.

As it was, Powel Crosley, Jr., was ready to retire. He had more than enough money to last another lifetime, and building small gasoline engines with his name on them held no glamour. He would soon turn 66, and no longer had the energy that had propelled him through successes (and failures) in the automotive, radio, broadcasting and home appliance industries. Truth be known, several personal tragedies plus the long downhill slide of Crosley Motors had robbed him of much of it.

A buyer for the company showed up almost immediately, eager to take over the government contract: the General Tire & Rubber Company. Newspaper reports stated that a controlling interest in Crosley Motors was purchased for a price that valued the auto company's shares at 20 cents each (for a total of $63,400). However, as with AVCO's purchase of the Crosley Corporation there were other elements to the deal. One of the conditions of the sale was that Powel Crosley be repaid the $3 million he had lent Crosley Motors. He also gained stock, and in a complicated deal was given ownership of some Crosley Motors property, which he leased back to General. After a merger of the two companies with the Aerojet Engineering Company (a major maker of rocket components) Crosley/General/Aerojet were reorganized as the Aerojet-General Company.

Aerojet obtained all the Crosley Motors plants, patents, designs, tools, material, inventory and other properties. Although the engine production was the main attraction in the deal, Aerojet did make use of the Crosley's Richmond factory, converting it to produce parts for jet-assisted takeoff (JATO) units for military aircraft. Between that and the continuing production of the CIBA engine plant most Crosley blue-collar workers retained their jobs for a while.

Aerojet hoped to find a buyer for the Crosley Motors name and all associated automotive designs, tooling, parts and so on. A Japanese company approached Aerojet, but no deal was made. Meanwhile, Aerojet renamed the engine "Aerojet" and was busy experimenting with it, for example building a vertical version of the CIBA that it called the "VIP," for Vertical Inline Power plant. It was rotated 90 degrees when it was mounted on a boat, and could be used to steer the watercraft it powered.

In 1954, Abena Investment and Development Company of Tel Aviv, Israel, made a tentative deal with Aerojet-General to resume production of Crosley automobiles. The cars would be manufactured in Israel, using the existing tools, to be sold in the United States. This deal, too, fell through. All of Crosley Motors, including machine tools, supplies and parts, was eventually auctioned off.

Ed Herzog, a former Crosley dealer from New York, had earlier tried to make a deal with Aerojet to continue production of the Crosley, but the required financing couldn't be found. At the Crosley Motors auction in 1955, Herzog was able to buy the complete stock of Crosley parts. (unfortunately, the tooling was scrapped.) Herzog set up a business, Service Motors, that kept Crosley owners supplied with replacement parts for decades, and is probably responsible for many of the Crosleys still on the road today. (Crosley Automobile Club members estimate that at least 7,000 to 8,000 Crosleys survive, running or not.)

Postwar production was 83,881 vehicles. Combined with prewar production of 5,757, the total number of Crosleys manufactured comes to 89,638. The number of COBRA and CIBA engines combined could well have been over one million.

Around 1955 Aerojet sold the rights to the Crosley engine to Lou Fageol, of the Twin Coach bus manufacturing company of Kent, Ohio. While building marine engines, Fageol experimented with radical versions of the CIBA, including such things as a flat, opposed eight-cylinder engine. A version of the four-cylinder called the

The Crosley engines, COBRA and CIBA. The engine block on the left (dark gray) is a CIBA. The other block and the complete engine are COBRAs. *Photo by Bill Angert*

The Skorpion, a four-piece fiberglass body built to "bolt on" to the standard Crosley chassis. Within four months of its first showing in November 1951, 20 kits had been sold. *Photo courtesy of Steve Cowdin*

Elgin was built for use with Sears boats.

The Crofton Marine Engine Company of California bought out the Fageol operation around 1959. Crofton continued to sell Crosley engines as boat motors and to the military. Included in the purchase was Fageol's $2 million inventory, from which Crofton started selling CIBA parts. Also produced was what looked like an updated version of the Farm-O-Road, powered of course by the CIBA. It was called the Crofton Bug.

With a 63-inch wheelbase, six forward speeds and two reverse, and options such as a winch, dual rear wheels and a vinyl roof/body enclosure, it was a direct descendent of the Farm-O-Road. For $200 extra, Crofton buyers could get a 53-cubic-inch version of the CIBA that produced 45 horsepower. This model was called the "Brawny Bug."

About 200 Crofton Bugs were produced. At least one "flatbed" version, called the Crofton Tug, was also built. After Crofton, CIBA production rights passed through the hands of several manufacturers, the last two Homelite and then Bearcat, up through 1972. (Special thanks to Jim Bollman for the factual details on the post-Crosley CIBA. Much more information is available at the Crosley Automobile Club Web site.)

The Crosley Hotshot and Super Sports continued racing for many years; some still turn up in old-timer rallies and formula races. Countless Crosley automobiles of all types have been modified to suit their owners' fancies. The modifications ranged from giving a Hotshot a grille, to customizing Crosley bodies to look like everything from miniature fuel tanker trucks to diesel railroad engines.

Brochure cover for the Skorpion. *Image courtesy of Steve Cowdin*

Crosley chassis often have been equipped with entirely new sports-car bodies. Long before the "dune buggy" body was developed for the Volkswagen, a small industry of aftermarket fiberglass bodies grew up around the Crosley, thanks to the popularity of sports cars and the ready availability of used Crosleys at low prices.

The most famous of these bodies was the Skorpion. Produced from 1950 through 1953, the Skorpion body was designed by Ralph Roberts (famous designer with Le Baron) and marketed by Viking-Craft. It was sold in kit form and as a completed car. There was also a Super

A Skorpion publicity shot. *Photo courtesy of Steve Cowdin*

Customized Skorpion with added grille. *Photo supplied by Steve Cowdin*

Skorpion, designed for the Crosley, Morris Minor and Renault 4CV chassis.

In addition to the Skorpion, bodies that could be mounted on a Crosley chassis included a body by the Clearfield Plastics Company, and its descendent, the Almquist Sabre, a beautifully-styled body that was the first of several from Almquist Engineering.

Crosley and the 750cc CIBA inspired more than one small carmaker. There was Nash's Rambler, of course, and later the Metropolitan. Willys and Hudson offered their own small cars in 1952, the Aero and the Jet. Both of these were larger than the Crosley, with 108- and 105-inch wheelbases, respectively. The Aero was well-appointed, with the heater standard. It sold through 1955. Just about every amenity on the Jet was an option. It lasted less than two years. Together with the Rambler, they seem to have proved George Mason's theory that small-car buyers did not want stripped-down vehicles.

Small Cars, Inc., in Kansas City built a fiberglass-bodied two-seater in 1955. The Crosley engine was to be one of the optional powerplants for the car. The company never went into production, and went under in 1956. Around the same time, Twin Coach built prototypes of a small car on a Renault chassis that likewise offered the CIBA engine as an option. It never went into production.

One of the myths about the Crosley is that it was inspired by the Volkswagen, or vice-versa. The Volkswagen followed its own, independent path of development on another continent where small cars were the norm. By the time Volkswagen reached North America in serious numbers (1955 in the U.S., and 1952 in Canada), the

Crosley was gone. But certainly Crosley had paved the way for all small cars.

As has been said often, Crosley Motors was just a little too early. Had the company sold more cars it might have lasted three more years, at which point small cars were catching on in the U.S. But Powel Crosley, Jr., seems to have missed or ignored the only things that might have sold more Crosleys, and which did sell Nash Ramblers: building a slightly larger car, and not offering stripped-down automobiles as economy cars.

The Metropolitan, Nash Rambler and VW carried the small-car torch into the late 1950s and early 1960s, and themselves prospered in an atmosphere in which bigger was better. That changed, of course, around the turn of the decade, when a new series of compact cars came to the market: the Chevrolet Corvair, Ford Falcon, Plymouth Valiant, Rambler American and Studebaker Lark. Eventually small cars would be a majority.

For a time at least, the Crosley had been a pleasant ride. Powel Crosley, Jr., had put nearly 90,000 cars on the highways of the world. Several were so innovative in design that people often see Crosley elements in to-day's automobile styling. And he achieved his dream of making new cars accessible to thousands of people who otherwise could not have owned one.

Powel Crosley, Jr., went on to lead a life of leisure. Having lost his first wife in 1939, he was again widowed, and twice more married and divorced. Dividing his time between his various properties in Cincinnati, Canada and South Carolina, he kept an eye on the Cincinnati Reds but contributed little to active management. He passed away early in 1961.

Postwar emblem. Cars had white jewels in front, red in rear.

Stylized version of Crosley coat of arms, on which emblem is based.

New emblem for 1949. *Photo by Bill Angert*

Crosley dealer banner. *Courtesy Bill Angert*

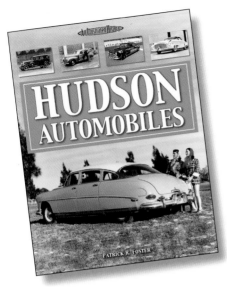

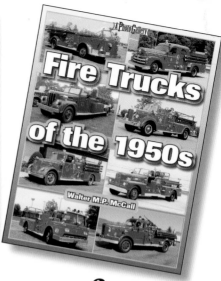

More Great Titles from Iconografix

All Iconografix books are available from specialty book dealers and bookstores worldwide, or can be ordered direct from the publisher. To request a FREE CATALOG or to place an order contact:

Iconografix
Dept BK
1830A Hanley Road
Hudson, WI 54016

Call:
(800) 289-3504
715-381-9755

Email: info@iconobooks.com

To see our complete selection of over 7,000 titles, visit us at:
www.enthusiastbooks.com
We would love to hear from you!

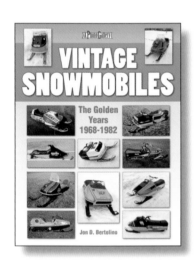

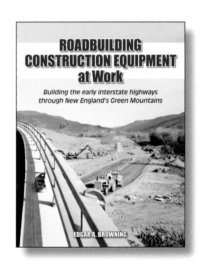

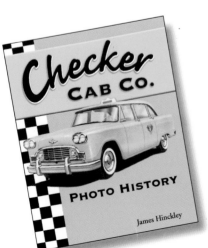

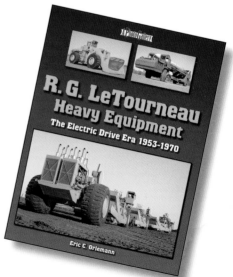